D0931662

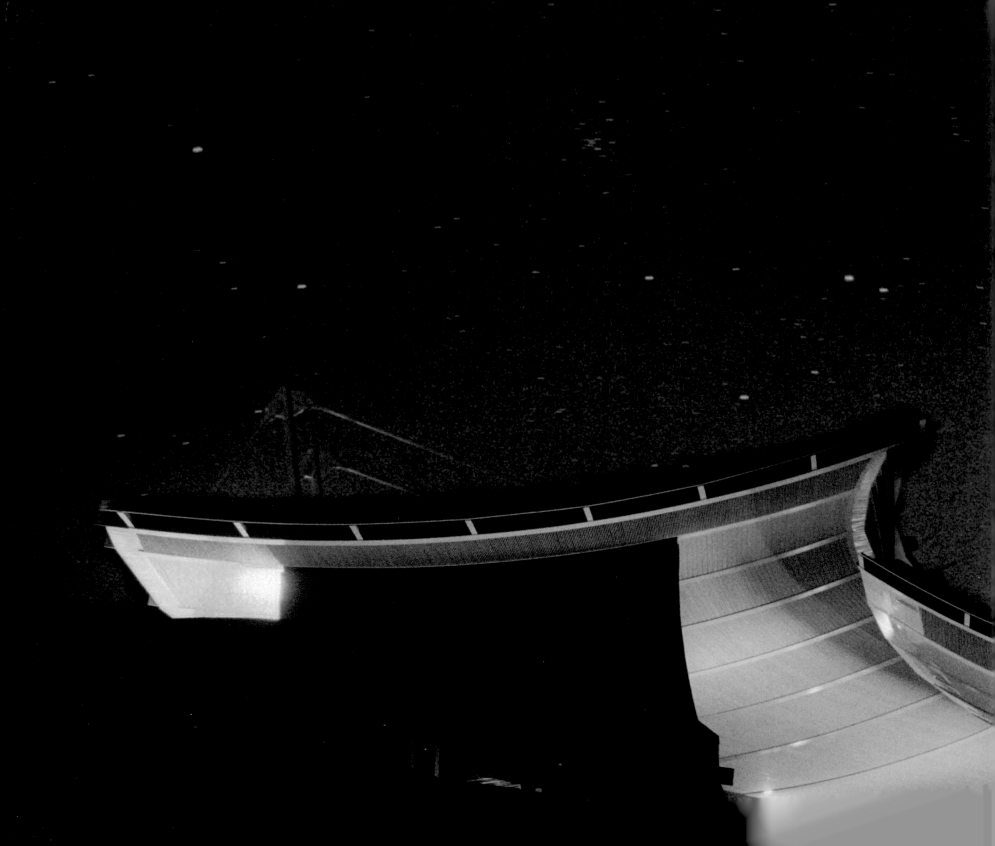

THE SANTA FE OPERA

AN AMERICAN PIONEER

PHILLIP HUSCHER

THE SANTA FE OPERA

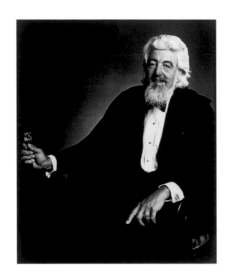

The Santa Fe Opera
is deeply grateful to
The Tobin Endowment
for underwriting this book,
which celebrates the
long friendship between
Robert L. B. Tobin and
John Crosby.

CONTENTS

VENUS AND ADONIS
Hans Werner Henze
2000

PROLOGUE

Driving north from Santa Fe, New Mexico, today, you are still met with what Juan de Oñate and the first Spanish explorers saw some four hundred years ago—what D. H. Lawrence later called "the big, unbroken spaces": a majestic expanse of distant mountains and ruler-top mesas, rumpled hills and arroyos, and a seemingly endless sky, sometimes brushed by clouds but often just pure, blinding blue. This is one of the most breathtaking of American landscapes, and because of its desolate terrain (in the high mountain desert) and its remoteness (at the edge of the American Southwest), it is as unlikely a site for a major opera house as you can imagine. For the past half century, The Santa Fe Opera house has sat on a low hill in the foreground of this panorama, and the juxtaposition of its dazzling, sculptural theater and the hardscrabble land—the totally modern and the very ancient, a state-of-the-art facility in a timeless setting—is as unexpected as the pairing of opera and the American West itself.

The birth of opera and the founding of Santa Fe share a page on the calendar—an upper-crust European entertainment and a frontier settlement springing to life at the same time. Early in 1598, *Dafne*, the first opera in history, was premiered in the Florentine palazzo of the wealthy merchant and arts patron Jacopo Corsi. On July 11 of that year, some six thousand miles away in the arid mesas of the New World, Oñate and his struggling troop of men reached the Indian pueblo of Ohkay Owingeh, just north of what now is Española, New Mexico. He would later rename it San Juan de los Caballeros, making it the first Spanish capital in this unexamined land.

These unrelated developments are part of a bigger picture, for the years around 1600 were a time of widespread discovery and innovation—a bridge from the Middle Ages to a modern world. Caravaggio painted his dramatically lit canvases, surprisingly cinematic to us today; Shakespeare, having emerged from his "lost years," gave us a *Hamlet* of deeply modern introspection; the new dance theater called Kabuki was named with a Japanese word meaning "unorthodox," "cutting edge"; Cervantes's *Don Quixote* posed the question we still ask: Who is man? The world seemed to expand; even the sky seemed wider. In 1609, Galileo Galilei built the first complete telescope so that he could study the Milky Way, the surface of the moon, sunspots, and planets—the same faraway objects that American Indians had long observed and worshiped, planting their crops according to the patterns of the night skies.

These new twin frontiers of art and exploration quickly established lasting roots. In Italy in 1607, Monteverdi's *Orfeo* became opera's first masterwork. It is the earliest opera still in the repertory today. In 1609, Spanish colonial official Pedro de Peralta established Santa Fe as the new capital of the territory and began laying the foundation of the Palace of the Governors. It is the oldest surviving non-Indian building in the United States. Today, that earthbound structure, often battered and rebuilt over the years as it housed a succession of rulers, shelters the north side of Santa Fe's Plaza—its broad portal now regularly lined with Native American artisans from nearby pueblos sitting in its shade, selling jewelry to the crowds of visitors who have made modern-day Santa Fe one of America's tourist meccas.

Today, The Santa Fe Opera is a festival of international importance. Inspired by the ideal of an American style of opera, the company has always had its own way of doing things. Its first star wasn't a great diva but a living composer, Igor Stravinsky, whose annual visits during the company's early years drew international attention. At a time when opera singers were more famous than opera composers, that was an important signal of the festival's priorities. The eyes of the operatic world soon shifted from the big cities to this little, out-of-the-way place where important moments in American musical history were taking place—the first productions in this country of Alban Berg's final masterpiece, *Lulu,* and Richard Strauss's last opera, *Capriccio;* the U.S. debuts of soon-to-be-superstars Kiri Te Kanawa and Bryn Terfel. Frederica von Stade, Thomas Hampson, Susan Graham, and Ben Heppner made early appearances in Santa Fe; Samuel Ramey, Neil Shicoff, and James Morris rose from the ranks of its apprentices. A company that proudly established itself without major names soon began to attract them:

Marilyn Horne and Natalie Dessay both came to Santa Fe at the peak of their fame. Over the years, The Santa Fe Opera made a steady practice of trying out untested operas, supporting young American singers on the threshold of important careers, courting major composers instead of big stars, and exploring the off-beat.

Like Bayreuth in the green hills of Wagner's Germany or Glyndebourne in the pastoral English countryside, The Santa Fe Opera became a place of pilgrimage—a destination for both performers and audiences. Still, Santa Fe has its own distinctive profile that sets it apart from all the summer festivals and big-league opera companies. It has never aspired to the glamour of Salzburg, the seriousness of Bayreuth, or the exclusivity of Glyndebourne. Santa Fe's objectives are distinctly American, and by making opera more compelling and more relevant, it has changed the map of musical America in fifty years. Perhaps, as Stravinsky suspected, it is because the company was founded by young people that it was driven from the start by the very idea of *possibility*—the possibility of doing things differently, of changing preconceptions, of exploring the new. Some of what The Santa Fe Opera has done has already gone down in the annals of opera; many of its accomplishments are forward-looking, even daring. Today, sitting proudly under Galileo's sky in the Hubble era, the company continues to work its magic.

THE BARBER OF SEVILLE
Gioachino Rossini
1981

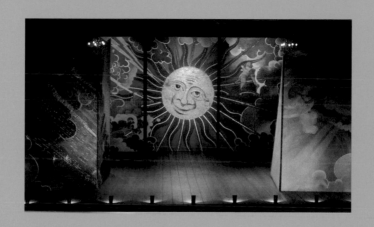

A NIGHT AT
THE OPERA

Tailgaters enjoy their
suppers and the view.

Each year, sometime around the first of July, The Santa Fe Opera opens its season. This has become a beloved tradition. Early in the evening, traffic backs up on the slow road to the parking lot, where Mercedes sedans and VW campers sit side by side with sleek limos, a 1939 Chevrolet flatbed, a lovingly restored vintage Packard and Hudson, a 1952 Ford pickup painted with sunflowers. Out come the plastic chairs and folding tables, fancy candlesticks, crystal goblets and the family silver, linen tablecloths and plastic champagne glasses. Tailgate parties have become part of the Opera experience—not just on opening night, but all season long—and sometimes the menus are even determined by the musical fare: chicken Kiev and Russian vodka for *Eugene Onegin,* Peking duck for *Turandot.*

Opening night is an occasion for theatrical attire—Venetian masks and canes, top hats and cowboy hats, concha belts and diamonds, Japanese silk wedding kimonos, leather miniskirts, aloha shirts—alongside traditional black tie and couture gowns. In the mid-seventies, Fritz Scholder, the Native American artist who then lived in Galisteo, south of Santa Fe, arrived in a dove-gray Lincoln stretch limo, wearing a black opera coat lined with purple that he had bought in Paris.

An evening spent at The Santa Fe Opera is in itself a dramatic event, beginning with the drive in from town, facing one of the most extraordinary backdrops in American scenery, on stage or off. At every turn, from the entrance plaza—the outdoor foyer where people mingle before the opera and linger under the stars at intermission—to the view from your seat

Dinner under a portal.

Dining before the opera
at the Cantina.

The Opera's dramatic entrance welcomes patrons.

inside, you know that you are in the high desert mountains. To the west, beyond the Rio Grande, the Jemez Mountains cut a jagged line across the horizon, deepening in color as they wait to swallow the setting sun. On the east, the gentle Sangre de Cristo range, capped by a glimpse of "Santa Fe Baldy," 12,622 feet high, rolls right down into town in velvety lumps. Looking north, you can see all the way to Colorado: San Antonio Mountain, some ninety miles away, rises near the state line. The prominent low ridge of Black Mesa, which Georgia O'Keeffe loved to paint, and the red outcropping of the Barrancas lie in the foreground.

One goes for the pleasure of hearing music, seeing powerful stage pictures, and enjoying compelling theater and ends up reveling in the entire experience. A Santa Fe audience is different from any other opera public in this country: a disarming mix of sharp-tongued opera fanatics and wide-eyed first-timers, music students with their dog-eared scores, elegantly tanned summer residents, footsore tourists, local families, would-be cowboys, real-life ranchers, and even the occasional celebrity. They come from everywhere—from all fifty states, from Canada, Japan, Europe, and South America—and from just down the road.

The opera begins at sunset—9 o'clock in July, then 8:30, and ultimately 8:00 as August wanes—which means that lengthy works like *Der Rosenkavalier* may not end till after midnight. That is the price of putting an open-air theater on a hill facing west, but it has of course also proved to be one of the benefits of going to the opera in Santa Fe, a town that is famous for sunset watching and for its dazzlingly crowded starry skies. Operagoers often arrive two or more hours

The audience gathers
before a performance.

Orchestra members
backstage before
a performance.

Anne Peterson warms up
in the orchestra pit.

before the performance begins, to picnic or to take in a pre-opera talk, or simply to people watch, gawk at the scenery, and make bets on the caliber of the approaching sunset. The pre-performance show is sometimes nearly as good as the opera itself, but this is an opera house where the wait is justified by what you are there to see.

Backstage, the hour before the opera starts is a time of anticipation. Stagehands, all dressed in "invisible" black, play bocce on the cement pier that drops off dramatically into the piñon-dotted hills—a line dividing the natural and the man-made, reality and illusion. Members of the crew sit on the long flight of steps leading down from stage level, chatting or reading in the fading

John Lofton practices
on the backstage deck.

•

(opposite)

Gregory Kunde, Celena Shafer, and Susan Graham on the backstage deck before *Lucio Silla,* 2005.

light. An occasional orchestra member wanders out back to warm up before settling in the pit. Half an hour before the top of the show, the various crews meet on the back steps to go over the evening's issues—whatever it is that needs special attention, a litany of all the things that dare not go wrong. A faint crescent moon—Galileo's moon—slowly rises like a giant *fermata,* as Federico García Lorca called it, suspended over this vast scene. Singers emerge from their dressing rooms, in full makeup and costume, to stand quietly and watch storms gathering in the distance or the glowing, deepening colors as the sun begins to slink down toward the Jemez Mountains.

And then, at sunset, the opera begins.

Backstage, apprentice
technicians assist Turandot
as she enters the stage, 2005.

Slippers await the barefoot
cast of *Ainadamar*, 2005.

LANDSCAPE NO. 3
(CASH ENTRY MINES, NEW MEXICO)
Marsden Hartley

SETTING
THE STAGE

Mabel Dodge Luhan (pictured with her husband Tony) was responsible for a major migration of artists to Taos and Santa Fe during the 1920s.

On a clear, bright day in 1956, Jack Purcell fired a rifle on the New Mexico desert hilltop where a young man named John Crosby wanted to build an opera house. Purcell, an acoustician from Boston, continued to fire shots, each time from a different spot, until he found the place where the explosive, echoing sound suggested a natural setting for an outdoor arena-like theater.

Fifteen-year-old John Crosby first came to New Mexico in 1941, when he was shipped off from his family home in comfortable Bronxville, New York, to attend school in Los Alamos, where his doctor thought the dry air of the high desert would relieve his asthma. Near the end of the school year that May, when he rode up the south side of Pajarito Peak in full sun and then descended the north side in snow up to his horse's belly, he realized that he had fallen in love with this wild and unpredictable place, so unlike the sheltered suburbs of Westchester County.

"There is something savage, unbreakable in the spirit of the place out here," D. H. Lawrence wrote in 1922, when he came to New Mexico at the urging of Mabel Dodge Luhan. Artists of a certain sensibility are drawn, sometimes despite themselves, to this particularly lush yet scruffy corner of the American Southwest, with its endless horizons and intense, pure, dazzling light, which a sixteenth-century Spaniard compared to a diamond. When Mabel Dodge came to New Mexico in 1917, she found "a new world that replaced all the

Mabel Dodge Luhan (pictured with her husband Tony) was responsible for a major migration of artists to Taos and Santa Fe during the 1920s.

ways I had known." A wealthy New Yorker by birth, Mabel already had reigned over celebrated salons in Florence, Italy, and in New York City, where for three years her Greenwich Village apartment at 23 Fifth Avenue was the most famous Wednesday night gathering place in America. In New Mexico, Mabel found a new husband (her fourth, the Taos Pueblo Native American Antonio Luhan) and tried to build yet another "cosmos" of artists and thinkers that would serve as a bridge between cultures. Even more ambitious than those in Florence or New York, her Taos salon attracted painters John Marin, Marsden Hartley, and Georgia O'Keeffe; the photographer Ansel Adams; the conductor Leopold Stokowski; the writers Robinson Jeffers, Willa Cather, and, of course, Lawrence.

Like Mabel Dodge, John Crosby came from a background so privileged and so quintessentially East Coast that his conversion to the freedom of New Mexico was as swift as it was improbable. He was born in New York in 1926. His father, Laurence Alden Crosby, was a law partner at Sullivan and Cromwell. His mother, Aileen O'Hea, a professional violinist and a chemist, taught him to play the violin and the piano. He studied at The Hotchkiss School for a year before being sent to the Los Alamos Ranch School, shortly before its facility was taken over for the Manhattan Project in 1943 during World War II. (Like Crosby, J. Robert Oppenheimer, who directed the nuclear weapons research in Los Alamos,

THUNDER DANCING
B. J. O. Nordfeldt

John Sloan spent
thirty-one summers painting
in and around Santa Fe.

became attached to New Mexico when he was sent there as a sickly young man.) Even after Crosby returned to Hotchkiss the next year, he kept coming back to New Mexico, because he couldn't get the place out of his system. His parents subsequently bought a summer home up on Tano Road, a few miles north of Santa Fe.

Crosby was a trained musician, and during World War II, when he served with the First Infantry Division, he played piano, violin, trombone, accordion, and double bass in the Eighteenth Regiment band. After the war was over, he went to Yale University, where he studied composition with Paul Hindemith, one of the few living composers of international stature teaching in the United States at the time. During summers in Maine, he took conducting lessons from Pierre Monteux, who had presided over the infamous Paris premiere of Stravinsky's *Rite of Spring* in 1913. At Yale, Crosby fell in love with Broadway musicals—he arranged the scores for college shows and attended Broadway tryouts in New Haven—and after he studied conducting at Columbia University in 1951 and began to play piano for Leopold Sachse's opera classes, he developed a sudden passion for opera.

While in New York, Crosby became a regular standee at the old Metropolitan Opera at 39th and Broadway, taking in the glories of America's operatic standard-bearer nearly every night of the week—this was the beginning of the Rudolf Bing era, and the golden age of old-school singers such as Zinka Milanov and Jussi Björling. But when Bing

unveiled the now-famous Alfred Lunt production of Mozart's *Così fan tutte*, sung in English and starring Eleanor Steber and Richard Tucker, Crosby saw something happen on the stage of the Met that he had never seen before: a "carefully, brilliantly rehearsed evening with six superb singing actors." That, he later realized, was the spark that inspired The Santa Fe Opera—it was the kind of opera that he wanted to present. Remote, taciturn, and soft-spoken, Crosby did not fit the conventional mold of an opera impresario or a cultural leader, but as it turned out, his seriousness, his single-mindedness, his attention to detail, and even his legendary, slow-boiling temper proved to be indispensable qualities in rethinking the way opera was produced in this country.

In the mid-fifties, when Crosby's ideas were taking shape, there were three major opera companies in the United States. Aside from the occasional oasis such as the Tanglewood and Ravinia festivals or the Cincinnati and Central City opera companies, little serious music of any kind was performed in the summer. Many orchestras stopped playing; most opera houses closed. Even artists' managers shut their offices and went to Europe. Crosby was particularly troubled that American singers had little choice but to take jobs in Europe during the summer, and he began to dream of a way to break that pattern.

Crosby knew that Santa Fe had a long tradition of what he called "hospitality to the arts" and that it was already

CHAMA RUNNING RED
John Sloan

THE SANTA FE TO
ALBUQUERQUE ROAD
Edward Weston

an established tourist destination, owing in no small part to Fred Harvey's Indian Detours promotions, which were headquartered at La Fonda Hotel, at the corner of the Plaza. Although painters, writers, sculptors, and photographers had formed a kind of colony there over the years, music, oddly, was missing. It was William Primrose, the well-known violist who recently had moved to Santa Fe, who ultimately told him, "If you don't start something here, John, somebody else will." Santa Fe was a town of some thirty thousand people in 1956, but it was home to a disproportionately large community of professional artists, including Primrose, the poet Witter Bynner, and the duo-pianists Vitya Vronsky and Victor Babin. "You felt the presence of the giants," Crosby said, not knowing at the time that he would soon entice more to the area.

Outside the town on the road north to Taos, just beyond his parents' home, an old ranch had come on the market. Early in the century, it had been farmed to grow pinto beans and then, with the addition of a few primitive buildings, to raise silver, blue, and red foxes. In the thirties, after a suspicious nighttime fire destroyed the structures—an eerie premonition of a later fire on the hill above—it became a pig farm. The San Juan Ranch, as it was known when Crosby looked at it, had recently been a summer guest ranch, with a main house that included a gracious central lounge with a big fireplace, a wing of bedrooms along a deep portal, and a kidney-shaped swimming pool. The owners had decided to put the property up for sale after the construction of a new highway just to the east of the ranch in 1956 put an end to its seclusion and quiet. Crosby immediately recognized it as an ideal headquarters for his opera company, with accommodations for visiting artists and a natural setting for an arena-like theater on a knoll above the ranch house. And, of course, he saw the highway as a distinct advantage for bringing in the crowds.

He immediately asked his father for a loan of $200,000 to buy the land and to build a theater, which he figured would cost $115,000. In the autumn of 1956, Crosby invited five local business leaders, including attorneys Thomas Catron and Robert Taichert, to lunch so that he could tell them about his plans for a new opera company in Santa Fe. Crosby had fleshed out his vision in painstaking detail—eighteen single-spaced typed pages, itemizing the projected costs for the first season down to the dry-cleaning bills for chorus costumes. The group was so impressed by his enthusiasm and financial savvy that their initial surprise and skepticism turned to outright excitement. The articles of incorporation were soon drawn up and a board of directors selected. Taichert became the first president and Catron would stay active in the company's affairs for the next five decades. Over the years, many others championed Crosby's vision and supported the company in critical times, among them Marshall and Perrine McCune, and Peggy Driscoll, whose continuing generosity ensured The Santa Fe Opera of today.

SANTA FE HILLS
Leon Kroll

RED HILLS WITH
THE PEDERNALES
Georgia O'Keeffe

What Crosby had outlined was nothing short of a revolution in American opera. In 1956, opera in this country was an imported luxury item. For decades, companies had clung to the ideal of European grand opera, with big-name casts and lavish productions designed to please a dressy society audience—a phenomenon virtually unchanged since Edith Wharton's portrait of opera in late-nineteenth-century New York City in *The Age of Innocence*. These rituals of etiquette and repertory persisted into the twentieth century and suggested the blueprint for new companies in San Francisco and Chicago. Opera in America had become a rather homogenized product, indistinguishable from what was presented in Vienna, London, or Paris.

Nothing about Crosby's plan followed the European model. The rural setting, in remote New Mexico, broke with the convention of putting opera houses at the heart of major urban cultural centers. And the theater he envisioned was not in the European historical tradition that favored stone facades, crushed-velvet seats, plaster cherubs, and engraved composer names. Instead, Crosby planned to build a simple, open-air theater of redwood and steel.

In addition, Crosby wasn't interested in international stars; he wanted to work with young American singers who would come together to create an ensemble. And he wanted to offer something beyond the classics. During the bitterly cold winter of 1956–57, while Crosby was planning the repertory for his new company, the Metropolitan Opera presented twenty-seven operas, all familiar works from the German, French, and Italian repertory, and, with the single exception of Richard Strauss's *Arabella*, which had been premiered in 1933, not one of them dated from the past fifty years. That winter, neither the San Francisco Opera nor the two-year-old Lyric Opera of Chicago featured a work written in this country or composed more recently than Riccardo Zandonai's *Francesca da Rimini*, which was first performed in Turin, Italy, in 1914. Crosby wanted to start a company that was modern in spirit, not nostalgic or old-fashioned. He saw The Santa Fe Opera as a center for a living art form—a reminder that people are still composing operas, and that opera still matters.

MUSIC IN THE PLAZA
John Sloan

JOHN CROSBY
IN REHEARSAL,
CIRCA 1960.

BRINGING
MUSIC TO THE
SILENT HILLS

Miranda Masocco Levy
and John Crosby greet
the Stravinskys at Lamy,
New Mexico.

"I always remember that Sunday morning in cold January 1957 . . . [when] you telephoned the Stravinskys and made everything happen," John Crosby wrote to Miranda Masocco Levy shortly before he died. Miranda was one of the young Santa Feans who supported Crosby and shared his excitement at starting a new opera company in their quiet little town. Miranda had met Igor and Vera Stravinsky in 1950, and she had immediately become a close friend, even sharing their box at the Metropolitan Opera premiere of the composer's *The Rake's Progress*, which Crosby considered one of the greatest operas of the twentieth century and wanted to stage during the first season in Santa Fe. Realizing that Crosby needed an important name to give prestige and credibility to his new venture, Miranda dialed the most prized number in her personal phone book that January morning, and she quickly got Stravinsky's attention, if not a firm commitment.

A few weeks later, Miranda, armed with blueprints and budgets, flew to Los Angeles to seal the deal. She raved about Crosby's talent and dedication. The composer was charmed by the idea of young people starting an opera company from scratch, but he was skeptical, fearing that the venture would be jeopardized by its remote location, the high altitude, the lack of tourists, the sparse population, or the unpredictable weather. Finally, he asked to see a photo of the opera house. Miranda calmly told him it wasn't built yet but would be ready for the opening in early July. Stravinsky agreed to come to Santa Fe anyway.

John Crosby spent two summers recording nighttime temperatures and studying prevailing winds, echoes, and sound patterns, and then hired local architects John McHugh and Van Dorn Hooker. They designed an outdoor theater seating 500 patrons on folding chairs and wooden benches, facing a covered stage with redwood walls and a series of sliding panels at the back that framed spectacular views of the Jemez Mountains to the west. A shallow, crescent-shaped reflecting pool, separating the audience from the orchestra pit, helped the acoustics.

Rehearsals began during the winter in New York City, where Crosby and most of the singers lived. Thomas Catron remembers Crosby calling him very early one morning from New York: "Listen to this," he said, and then put the phone down so Catron could hear a rehearsal for *Madame Butterfly,* which was to open the season. That morning, for the first time, Catron realized what Crosby was capable of—that this was a major enterprise. Crosby showed up in Santa Fe on June 1, moved into the San Juan Ranch house, and set to work preparing for opening night, just a month away. Nothing escaped his attention, and he jumped in wherever he was needed, from planting white petunias on the theater patio (chosen so they could be seen at night) to driving to

John Crosby marking a score
during rehearsal, 1959.

Denver to pick up transformers for the lighting system's dimmer bank.

Construction was completed in time for the opening on July 3, despite delays and last-minute snafus. (Crosby was working on the theater plumbing that night, just before he changed into his conducting clothes.) "The traffic on the big, four-lane Santa Fe–Taos highway was fin to fender one evening last week," *Time* magazine reported in its coverage of The Santa Fe Opera that summer. The opening night performance of Puccini's *Madame Butterfly*, with Crosby in the pit, fully justified his extraordinary gamble. There were ten curtain calls, and the next day United Press International reported, "There was nothing amateur about it," which is perhaps what most surprised the out-of-town reporters, aside from the sheer novelty of seeing opera under an open western sky studded with stars. *Time* wondered if Santa Fe would become the "Salzburg of the Southwest," raising for the first time the comparison with the venerable Austrian festival that would prove apt in a surprisingly short time. The first six performances sold out, the crowds continued to come all summer long—tickets were sensibly priced at $2.40, $3.60, and $4.80—and it was estimated that 70 percent of the audience that season had never before attended an opera. Gustave Baumann, whose woodcuts are among the most evocative depictions of classic Santa Fe, wrote in *The New Mexican:* "My hat's off to John Crosby, who was able to see something where there was nothing before and who brought sweet sound to the silent hills."

In the early days, the terrace was the scene for a variety of activities.

Nearly everyone in the company that first summer was under thirty; Crosby turned thirty-one on July 12, nine days after the opening. There were sixty-seven artists on the payroll. Not one of the leading singers was a superstar, but they were all what Crosby called "total" artists—"actors, singers, musicians, minds that go to work"—most of them drawn from the ranks of the New York City Opera, the NBC Opera Company, and the Lyric Opera of Chicago. Regina Sarfaty, who sang Suzuki in the opening night *Butterfly*, was twenty-two and just beginning a career that would take her all over the world and bring her back to Santa Fe forty years later to work with apprentices. Although she eventually sang more than four hundred performances of *Butterfly*, this was the one she would remember most fondly. The thirty-four orchestra members came to Santa Fe from the Metropolitan Opera and the New York Philharmonic and from the Chicago, Houston, and Kansas City symphonies. Eleven apprentice singers "anxious to perfect their art by appearing in small roles with a professional group," as the 1957 program book stated, were the seed of the country's first training program for opera.

In its first season, The Santa Fe Opera produced seven operas, a highly ambitious agenda for a start-up venture, but one that also made it perfectly clear, from the scope and variety of the offerings, just what it wanted to accomplish. In addition to the inaugural *Butterfly*, Crosby picked only one other repertory staple—Rossini's *The Barber of Seville*.

An original Ranch building.

View of the entrance gate
to the first theater.

The balance of the season was a wonderfully diverse group of operas that were rarely performed in the 1950s. *Così fan tutte,* the work that had inspired Crosby to create a new kind of opera company in the first place, wasn't nearly as highly regarded at the time as the other two operas Mozart wrote with Lorenzo da Ponte, *Don Giovanni* and *The Marriage of Figaro.* Similarly, Strauss's *Ariadne auf Naxos* was hardly unknown, but it wasn't big box office like *Salome, Elektra,* and *Der Rosenkavalier.* Stravinsky's *The Rake's Progress* had been produced just once before in the United States, even though it was acknowledged as one of his most important scores. Pergolesi's delightful comedy *La serva padrona* was an unusual excursion into the world of opera before Mozart. And, sharing a double bill with Pergolesi was the world premiere of Marvin David Levy's *The Tower*—the presence of that single opera alone, a new American opera for a new American opera company, signaling that Santa Fe had its own way of doing things.

While Gaetano Merola, the founder of the San Francisco Opera, called that city "my other Italy," and Carol Fox maintained Chicago's Lyric as a predominantly "Italian" opera company for years, Crosby had no delusions about his company's geographical or cultural roots. For the first few seasons, all the operas were sung in English, which was unusual at the time and only helped to underline the company's intent to make opera more familiar.

The first season's repertory set the tone for the following years—a mixture of classics retold in fresh and exciting ways, modern works that needed to be heard, and, most daringly, the unknown. It was a sign of the company's personality and ambition. The opening season's *Ariadne* launched a focus on Strauss that would continue for many years. Stravinsky's participation evolved into an emphasis on living composers, many of whom, like Stravinsky, would come to Santa Fe—often from far away—to help bring their works to life under ideal conditions. The bold leap into the unknown with Levy's *The Tower* would be taken again every few seasons, occasionally with disappointing results, but more often happily.

From the start, Santa Fe's isolation worked to the company's advantage, enabling it to bring an ensemble of singers together for the entire summer in an unusually close-knit family atmosphere. Years later, Crosby admitted that he had the model of Wagner's Bayreuth Festival in the back of his mind, remembering that Wagner put his festival out in the country precisely so that the artists would be left alone to concentrate on preparation, and so that the public would make a pilgrimage.

Several major American newspapers and magazines sent critics out to Santa Fe, sensing that there was a good story and perhaps even great opera to be found in the hills of northern New Mexico. "The attention of the music world

Rudolf Bing and
John Crosby.

was focused last summer on one of the most phenomenal beginnings in U.S. operatic history," the critic from *Opera News* wrote in October. "By the end of its two-month season, Santa Fe had joined the ranks of important festivals and broken all records for speed in establishing a tradition."

Ironically, it was Rudolf Bing who made it clear, however, that Santa Fe still faced an uphill battle before it would be considered in the front rank of U.S. companies. "There is no opera in America worth speaking of outside New York City," he said in an interview that October, conceding, when pressed, that Chicago and San Francisco also demanded attention. When the reporter wondered what he thought about the new Santa Fe company, he asked, "Where is Santa Fe?" The remark outraged Santa Feans ("Who's Bing?" Mayor Leo Murphy shot back), embarrassed Bing, and made the current issue of *Time*. Crosby's response? The day the article hit the newsstands, he invited Bing to join the newly created artistic council of The Santa Fe Opera. *Time*'s next issue ran a follow-up on the Bing situation: "This week, with the location of Santa Fe firmly fixed in his mind, he accepted an invitation to join The Santa Fe Opera's advisory committee."

Bing recognized his folly and apologized, but his attitude wasn't unusual, and the company continued to receive comments about cow towns and horse operas in its glowing reviews. Nevertheless, The Santa Fe Opera was a great story, and it was soon mentioned not only in the musical press but in the major weeklies as well, including *Saturday Review*, and in the glossy monthlies, from *House and Garden* to *Vogue*.

When The Santa Fe Opera was founded, no opera companies in the United States were training young singers; Americans went to Europe to study and to get valuable stage experience. The eleven apprentice singers who took bit roles and doubled as a chorus that first season in Santa Fe broke the pattern. An aspiring baritone from Hinsdale, Illinois, could save his airfare and drive out to Santa Fe, where he could study diction, staging, and body movement; work with singers who had already "earned their spurs," in Crosby's Wild West metaphor; and even get a bit of onstage exposure. That was exactly what happened to Sherrill Milnes, the first of the Santa Fe apprentices to make it big, who joined the Opera's program in 1959 after studying with Rosa Ponselle, the reigning American soprano of the twenties and thirties. Milnes ended up singing small roles in two major productions that summer before beginning a fabled thirty-two-year career at the Met.

The program caught on immediately, and in 1967 more than three hundred singers from all over the country auditioned to be Santa Fe apprentices; by the 1980s, that number

A view of backstage and
the Sangre de Cristo
Mountains, 1957.

Vera Zorina coaches
apprentices for
Igor Stravinsky's
Perséphone, 1961.

had topped eight hundred. The competition was always tough, and it has only gotten stiffer, and each year's class not only suggests that the future of American opera is in good hands but also provides Santa Fe with one of the finest choruses anywhere—these singers are so stage savvy that they can easily become the villagers of Britten's *Peter Grimes,* the American townsfolk in *The Mother of Us All,* and seemingly all of Peking in *Turandot.*

The program was soon emulated, from Saint Louis to San Francisco and from Glimmerglass to Central City, and it is now considered an essential part of an American opera company's artistic profile. Just as Santa Fe was a pioneer in setting the agenda for the repertory of the future, it also was the first company in this country to put supporting the next generation of performers at the heart of its mission. This is arguably Santa Fe's most influential idea, and it quickly changed the way opera was produced in America. When Crosby was awarded a National Medal of the Arts by President George H. W. Bush in 1991—along with Grand Ole Opry star Roy Acuff and *A Night at the Opera* star Kitty Carlisle Hart—special attention was paid to his "dream of giving young American artists the opportunity to train and perform in their own country." In 1965, the company started a similar program for technicians wanting experience in lighting, costuming, scenery, or props. Many of them have gone on to jobs at the Met or Chicago's Lyric—or returned to Santa Fe.

The Santa Fe Opera style, with its strong emphasis on theater and well-rehearsed casts of American singers, quickly began to have an influence throughout the country, and it served as the model for an entire generation of regional opera companies. Eventually, some of Crosby's employees left Santa Fe to strike out on their own. David Gockley, who first came to Santa Fe as a baritone apprentice in 1965— he sang small roles in *Madame Butterfly* and *Carmen*—and then worked in the box office, left to study business administration at Columbia and was running the Houston Grand Opera at the age of twenty-seven. Charles MacKay played french horn in The Santa Fe Opera orchestra and then became the orchestra librarian and worked in the business office before he left for the Spoleto Festival in Charleston, South Carolina.

Richard Gaddes, who grew up in a small town in the north of England and studied at London's Trinity College of Music, came in 1969 to work at Crosby's right hand as the company's artistic administrator and soon proved to be an ideal complement to Crosby's style. Gaddes brought a wealth of musical knowledge and a wide range of experience to Santa Fe—he had his first brush with great music making when he turned pages for pianist Gerald Moore in Dietrich Fischer-Dieskau's lieder recitals; later on he established

A rehearsal at
O'Shaughnessy Hall,
1980s.

John Crosby and Robert L. B. Tobin.

a lunchtime concert series at London's Wigmore Hall and worked for a prominent artist management firm. In 1976, Gaddes was invited to start the Opera Theatre of Saint Louis, which was unapologetically indebted to the Santa Fe model.

He wasn't gone long. With the Saint Louis company up and running, Gaddes returned to Santa Fe as a consultant in the eighties and was named associate general director in 1995. Shortly afterward, it was announced that Gaddes would succeed Crosby, a transfer of power that seemed particularly logical and orderly—at the very time the Wagner family was publicly haggling over the future leadership of the Bayreuth Festival. Crosby stepped down at the end of the 2000 season, just after he turned seventy-four—his final act as the head of the company he founded was to conduct Strauss's *Elektra,* his 567th appearance on the Santa Fe podium. As Gaddes later pointed out, Rudolf Bing had once said that no one should lead an opera company past the age of seventy-five, and Crosby took that seriously. Although he returned to conduct the following two summers, he began spending more time in Palm Springs, where he bought a house and, as a retirement present to himself, a 1985 mint-condition, silver Rolls-Royce Corniche convertible with a carriage blue interior and hood.

John Crosby died unexpectedly in December 2002, following surgery for appendicitis. He had last appeared with the company conducting *La traviata* that August. On July 12 of the following summer, the date he had been scheduled to open Strauss's *Intermezzo* on what would have been his seventy-seventh birthday, a memorial service was held in the opera house that would from then on be known as the Crosby Theatre. Christine Brewer, who made her Santa Fe debut as Ariadne under Crosby's baton in 1999, sang the "Four Last Songs" by Crosby's beloved Richard Strauss.

Crosby had always looked to the examples of George Balanchine, whose name was once synonymous with the New York City Ballet, and Rolf Liebermann, who reigned over legendary eras at the Hamburg and Paris opera companies, saying that "the best artistic organizations are those that exist in the shadow thrown by their leaders." The Santa Fe Opera has flourished since Crosby's death because its foundation was so strong, the transition shrewdly paced, and the new leadership inspired.

Betty Allen, John Crosby, and
Vinson Cole discuss the score for
the 1975 production of *La vida breve*.

With Gaddes in charge, the Opera has managed a delicate balance of tradition and innovation, of continuity and breakthrough. Without losing sight of the company's original mission, he has begun to shift the repertory in new directions, to update the production standards, and to breathe new life into the casting. Gaddes quickly started thinking of ways to make opera more accessible, particularly to the local community, adding earlier performance times and pre-opera lectures, selling half-price tickets to first-timers, arranging shuttle transportation from Santa Fe and Albuquerque. In 2004, when the entire run of *La sonnambula* sold out almost overnight, he organized a free live telecast in Fort Marcy Park, close to the Plaza.

Gaddes also has overseen off-season productions of *The Beggar's Opera* and *H.M.S. Pinafore* in downtown theaters, which were a big hit with year-round residents. The Santa Fe community took the Opera to its heart the very first season, and it continues to play an unusually active role in the company's success. Today, guild chapters of volunteers in eight cities and more than one thousand local volunteers support educational activities that have been in place for years—the Pueblo Opera Program that brings

Apprentices relax on the lawn in the early 1970s.

residents of nineteen nearby pueblos and reservations to "Youth Nights" each summer; the Student Produced Opera Program that encourages young people from schools in central and northern New Mexico to write, produce, and perform their own operas; the annual springtime touring ensemble of apprentices, which performs around the state.

In 2003, Gaddes appointed young conductor Alan Gilbert as The Santa Fe Opera's first music director—someone not only to offer artistic leadership but also to oversee the long-term health of the orchestra, which is one of the great strengths of the company. The son of New York Philharmonic players, Gilbert is an accomplished violinist, a devoted chamber music player, and one of the most successful American conductors of his generation. Gilbert had already led *Falstaff* and *Eugene Onegin* in Santa Fe, but he has a strong Santa Fe connection, another bridge from past to future: Gilbert's father was a longtime concertmaster of the Opera orchestra, and Gilbert himself was assistant concertmaster in 1993. Under Gaddes, The Santa Fe Opera has found a way to stand in a historic shadow and at the same time to move ahead.

Richard Gaddes and
John Crosby confer at
the Cantina, 1975.

The simulcast of
La sonnambula in Fort Marcy
Park, Santa Fe, 2004.

Cochiti Pueblo
children in a
Student Produced
Opera Program
production, 2003.

Children perform in
Benjamin Britten's
Noah's Flood, 1996.

NORMAN BOYLES'S SCULPTURE
GRACES STRAVINSKY TERRACE.

STRAVINSKY
IN SANTA FE

(opposite)

John Crosby and Igor Stravinsky
watch a rehearsal of
The Rake's Progress, 1957.

Igor Stravinsky fell in love with New Mexico the day he arrived in 1950, traveling down from Aspen by car. He and his wife Vera had gone to Colorado that summer, driving from their home in Los Angeles via Yellowstone Park, so that he could conduct two concerts at the year-old Aspen Music Festival. Learning that Frieda Lawrence, the widow of D. H. Lawrence, now lived in Taos, New Mexico, just across the state line, Stravinsky organized a road trip. He and Vera rode down with Robert Craft, who had become his assistant two years earlier. They were joined by their friends, duo-pianists Vronsky and Babin, who had a house in Santa Fe and who had suggested that they put their itinerary in the hands of Miranda Masocco, who would meet them in Taos. They stopped first at Frieda's Kiowa Ranch, at the foot of the San Cristobal Mountains just north of Taos, where they had breakfast with Lawrence's widow and visited the chapel that housed his remains; they then continued on to the celebrated adobe "salon" of Mabel Dodge Luhan, who kept them waiting in the midday sun and then failed to impress the distinguished composer with her legendary charm.

Miranda, who in a single morning developed a keen sense of what made Stravinsky tick, suggested that they keep driving on south through Santa Fe in order to catch the end of the Tewa Indian Corn Dance at the Santo Domingo Pueblo. Despite the suffocating heat and the swirling dust, Stravinsky was entranced by the powerful ritualistic dancing, and when Miranda saw tears streaking his dusty face, she knew they would be soul mates for life. During the next three days in Santa Fe, the Stravinskys had a fine time and they quickly came to realize that this sleepy little town was an unusually cosmopolitan community. Seven years later, when Stravinsky picked up the phone in his Hollywood home and heard Miranda's alluring voice full of excitement at the prospect of a new opera company in the hills north of Santa Fe, he was flooded with fond memories.

On July 8, 1957, the Stravinskys arrived on the Super Chief at the station in Lamy, just south of Santa Fe, where they were met by Crosby. Rehearsals for *The Rake's Progress* were already under way. Stravinsky had suggested that Craft conduct the opera, which he knew better than anyone else. The opera was in good hands all around: the three principals were singers Stravinsky himself had chosen for the 1953 Boston production, and the Santa Fe director, Bliss Hebert, had overseen that staging. Over the next two weeks, Stravinsky was a larger-than-life presence at rehearsals, even though he tended to sit unobtrusively in the wings or at the

corner of the stage, with his head sometimes buried in the score, quietly making
suggestions or just observing. One night,
when Crosby was busy repairing a scenery
flat that had blown over just as rehearsal
started, he looked up to find that it was
Stravinsky who had been quietly handing him the screws
and holding the cloth in place.

The Rake's Progress was only six years old in 1957. From
the time of its premiere in Venice's historic La Fenice in 1951,
it was recognized as major Stravinsky—it is the longest of all
his scores, the crowning work of his neoclassic phase, and
the major landmark of his American years. But following the
indifferent reception it received at the Metropolitan Opera
in 1953, no American company had shown any interest in
staging the work. The 1957 Santa Fe Opera production gave
the opera a new lease on life, and at the end of the opening
night performance, Stravinsky was shouted to the stage to
share in the standing ovation.

Over the next few seasons, Santa Fe began to build an
audience for Stravinsky's masterwork. By the time of its 1962
production, its third staging in five years, it was playing to
sold-out houses. "In Santa Fe," the no-nonsense critic and
composer Virgil Thomson wrote that year, "garage mechanics

(opposite)

Igor Stravinsky conducts
a rehearsal of
Oedipus rex, 1960.

and their wives have taken to their hearts,
believe it or not, Stravinsky's *The Rake's
Progress.*" For many years, Santa Fe was
the only American company that produced the opera regularly, helping to
establish its reputation as one of the
classics of twentieth-century opera.

The Stravinskys returned to Santa Fe five of the next six
summers. They often were on the road during these years,
but Santa Fe became a kind of second home to them. They
took the summer of 1958 off—the Opera wasn't presenting
any of the composer's works; instead, Stravinsky began the
first of his books of conversations with Craft. Again in 1959,
there was no Stravinsky on the Opera bill, but Craft was in
Santa Fe to conduct Donizetti's rarely staged *Anna Bolena*
and the Stravinskys came to town for an extended visit.

In July, Stravinsky conducted the American premiere of
Threni, his twelve-tone setting of the Lamentations of Jere-
miah, in the Cathedral of Saint Francis, capped by "two
earthen towers that rose high above the flatness," as Willa
Cather wrote in *Death Comes for the Archbishop.* The performance had needed a special dispensation from the archbishop of Santa Fe, Edwin Byrne—the successor to Jean
Baptiste Lamy, the subject of Cather's novel—for it broke with

Paul Hindemith and
Igor Stravinsky in Santa Fe
at the time of the American
premiere of Hindemith's
News of the Day, 1961.

church policy for a concert to be held in a sacred place. The Santa Fe cathedral concert drew a capacity audience, with loudspeakers set up outside for the overflow.

At the end of the season, Stravinsky wrote an enviable endorsement of The Santa Fe Opera, assisted by his new friend Paul Horgan, who had already won a Pulitzer Prize for a history of the Rio Grande and would later win another for *Lamy of Santa Fe*. Stravinsky praised the way his works had been presented there with taste and skill, and he wished the company "a long future of prosperity and further artistic achievement"—a future in which he played a key role.

Over the years, the Stravinskys became a familiar and friendly—though sometimes "imperial"—presence around town. After all, they were used to the world's luxuries (the Paris Ritz and the Hassler in Rome were regular haunts) and to receiving royal treatment wherever they went, but they quickly fell into the simple rhythm of daily life in Santa Fe. Stravinsky often could be spotted lunching under the cottonwoods in the patio at La Fonda, wearing the black beret Picasso had given him, or wandering the aisles of Woolworth's on the Plaza (he proudly bought rubber pads intended to keep his eyeglasses from slipping but then mounted them the wrong way). While Stravinsky worked, rehearsing at the

Opera or writing music at a muted piano in his hotel suite, Vera shopped or worked on her paintings. During his summers in Santa Fe, Stravinsky composed many of his last important works: Movements for piano and orchestra; *A Sermon, a Narrative and a Prayer; The Flood; Abraham and Isaac;* and the Aldous Huxley memorial Variations for Orchestra. One rare free day, they drove with Craft and Horgan to picnic amid the cliff dwellings and ruins at Bandelier National Monument, where, after enjoying a Portuguese rosé and a passing rain shower, Stravinsky suddenly seemed years younger.

Stravinsky was back in Santa Fe again in 1960, this time to conduct the Opera's production of his powerful *Oedipus rex* (with Horgan as the Narrator), which awkwardly shared a double bill with Puccini's sparkling comedy *Gianni Schicchi*. If Puccini nearly overshadowed Stravinsky—the comic opera was mentioned everywhere from *The Saturday Review* to *Harper's Bazaar*—it was because it starred the popular actor José Ferrer making his debut as an opera singer. (Ferrer was joined in town by his wife, singer Rosemary Clooney, and their children, who referred to his role, not altogether inaccurately, as Johnny Squeaky.) That summer, Stravinsky also supervised a new production of *The Rake's Progress,*

An orchestra rehearsal of Stravinsky's
The Rake's Progress at the Ranch.

OEDIPUS REX
Igor Stravinsky
1960

conducted by Craft, attending all of the rehearsals, shielded from the sun by a market umbrella during the day or wrapped in a scarf to cut the evening chill. In a second Cathedral Concert, he conducted his *Symphony of Psalms,* one of the monuments of modern choral music.

Stravinsky invited ballerina Vera Zorina to Santa Fe to appear as his Perséphone for the 1961 season. Zorina, the former wife of George Balanchine and a principal dancer in the Ballets Russes of Monte Carlo, was now married to Goddard Lieberson, the president of CBS Records. Zorina had made her name in the late 1930s, when movie mogul Samuel Goldwyn took her to Hollywood, where she made a string of popular films, including *The Goldwyn Follies, On Your Toes,* and *Louisiana Purchase.* Zorina, who already had recorded *Perséphone* under Stravinsky, brought a marvelous mixture of dancing, acting, speaking, and singing to the role. "This was the Perséphone I always dreamed of and never saw until now," Stravinsky said. Zorina came to Santa Fe that summer with her two children—one teenage son, Peter, would return to town thirty-six years later as the composer of *Ashoka's Dream,* which had been commissioned by the Opera—and she appeared with the company several times during the following years.

For the *Perséphone* costumes, the Opera wisely turned to Vera Stravinsky, who had designed costumes and painted scenery for Diaghilev's Ballets Russes in Paris. Vera was a woman of remarkable presence—her great eyes "lustrous with humor and immediate opinion," as Horgan wrote—and considerable skill as an abstract painter. Her work had been shown for the first time in New York in 1957, shortly before the couple came to Santa Fe for the summer. "She sees the heavenly oddity in things," Aldous Huxley wrote for the exhibition catalog. Her first Santa Fe show drew an illustrious art-world crowd, including legendary New York dealer Betty Parsons, New Mexican painter Randall Davey, the influential architect and designer Alexander Girard, painter Peter Hurd, and photographer Eliot Porter.

Following the Opera's 1961 season, *Oedipus rex* and *Perséphone,* conducted by the composer, along with *The Ballad of Baby Doe,* were performed in West Berlin and Belgrade on a tour sponsored by the U.S. State Department. The Santa Fe Opera was the first American opera company selected for this program.

In 1962, when Stravinsky turned eighty, The Santa Fe Opera produced all of his pieces written for the opera stage: *Mavra, Rénard,* and *Le rossignol* in a triple bill; *Oedipus rex,*

PERSÉPHONE
Igor Stravinsky
1961

Vera Zorina

Richard Gaddes (left) and
John Crosby (right) with
Robert Craft and Vera Stravinsky,
1972.

again more sensibly paired with *Persé-phone;* and *The Rake's Progress*—all in ten days. Stravinsky himself conducted *Le rossignol,* and Zorina repeated her success as Perséphone. At a third Cathedral Concert, featuring the composer's ten-year-old Cantata, Stravinsky received a long, silent embrace from Archbishop Byrne, who died later that year.

No other company in the world matched Santa Fe's Stravinsky Festival, as the congratulatory telegram from President John F. Kennedy made clear—"The Santa Fe Opera distinguished itself and honors a very great man by presenting the festival marking Igor Stravinsky's eightieth year," it began. Stravinsky was thrilled and genuinely touched. "Santa Fe," he said, "is my family. So the celebration here is like having my birthday party at home."

Stravinsky came to Santa Fe just one last time, in 1963, to conduct his Mass in a final Cathedral Concert. After the concert, Stravinsky was invested with the Papal Knighthood of Saint Sylvester, which he accepted to prolonged applause. The Stravinskys left for Los Angeles that night by car. Vera returned in 1972, a year after her husband's death, to unveil three commemorative plaques: at the Museum of Fine Arts, Saint Francis Cathedral, and The Santa Fe Opera. In 1998, the large terrace to the north of the Opera theater, with its views of the highway back up to Colorado, was named for Stravinsky. A small sculpture of his head, set at the far north end and lit by simple spotlights throughout performances, watches over the continuing work of the company he helped to put on the map.

LE ROSSIGNOL
Igor Stravinsky
1970

Gimi Beni
Betty Lane

THE RAKE'S PROGRESS
Igor Stravinsky
1996

Sylvia McNair
Richard Croft

(below)

Richard Croft
Josepha Gayer

(opposite)

THE RAKE'S PROGRESS
Igor Stravinsky
1966

Elaine Bonazzi
Donald Gramm

THE THIRD THEATER

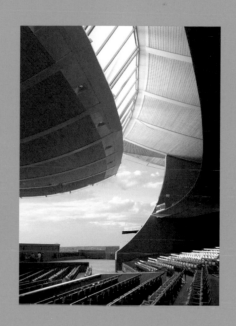

A HOUSE
FOR MUSIC

The staircase was all that
remained after the fire, 1967.

At 4:05 in the morning of July 27, 1967, Santa Fe dispatchers received a call that the Opera house was on fire. To this day, no one is certain how or when the blaze started, but firemen later found a watch left in a makeup room, stuck at 12:20, which made them wonder if the heat was already intense enough at that time to stop a clock. Georg Schreiber, the company lighting designer, who was staying in a house just below the Ranch, heard explosions in his sleep that sounded like the fireworks at the end of Henze's *The Stag King*. Realizing that the company hadn't staged the work in two years, he woke abruptly to find the theater engulfed in flames.

More than thirty firemen battled the fire, quickly emptying the three 750-gallon tanks they brought and then pumping a 10,000-gallon cistern dry. When the water ran out, there was nothing to do but watch. By dawn, all that remained were a few twisted girders and the concrete stairs leading to a new balcony that had been built during the winter of 1964–65, when the original theater was more than doubled in size and a partial roof was added.

The night before the fire, the company had given the American premiere of Hindemith's *Cardillac*. Ragnar Ulfung, the first European to appear with the company and an artist who would become a Santa Fe regular, sang "one of the last notes on the old stage," as he later put it. A good-luck charm made with his children's baby teeth and the wedding ring that he left behind in the dressing room were now lost in the ash and rubble, along with dozens of instruments, including a 232-year-old double bass once played at La Scala, and the company's inventory of sets and costumes, except for two boxes of feathers that mysteriously escaped the flames. Only the costumes for *The Barber of Seville,* which had just been sent to the cleaners, survived.

Crosby was one of the first people to arrive on the scene, and by the early hours of the morning he and Mrs. Walter M. "Peaches" Mayer, the near-legendary president of the board, had already assembled the staff and trustees to come up with a plan of action.

Santa Feans were devoted to their young opera company and were quick to come to its aid. Robert L. B. Tobin, a board member who owned survey planes, sent one of them to San Antonio, Texas, to bring back instruments, two sets of orchestral parts for the Rossini opera, and forty-five music stands with lights that belonged to the San Antonio Symphony. By noon the day after the fire, Mag Tobin, Robert's mother, set up a costume shop in the living room of her home on Camino del Monte Sol; other local residents donated props and clothes; many opened their checkbooks. St. John's College, its Santa Fe campus just three years old, turned a big fund-raiser that was originally planned

Construction begins
on the backstage, 1967.

for its own library into a benefit for the Opera.

A second performance of *Cardillac* scheduled for the following night was scrapped. A makeshift *Barber of Seville* took its place, staged at the local high school's Sweeney Gymnasium, with impromptu sets, borrowed props, imported double basses, and a thumb-nailed piano passing for a harpsichord. Before the performance, when Crosby spoke to the crowd of 1,300, he was interrupted by six minutes of rhythmic clapping. The rest of the summer season went on in the gymnasium as scheduled. The performance of *La bohème* on Saturday was played, by necessity, in modern dress, followed by the American premiere of Henze's *Boulevard Solitude* on Wednesday night to a packed house. New orchestral parts, now the only set in existence, had been flown in from Frankfurt, Germany.

Stravinsky agreed to serve as national chairman of a campaign that eventually raised nearly $2 million for the rebuilding of the theater. The Santa Fe Opera now unexpectedly joined a wave of new performing arts centers being built across the country, from New York's Lincoln Center to the first stages of a cultural complex in downtown Los Angeles. After three hundred working days and despite heavy winter snowstorms, the new Santa Fe Opera

The McHugh-designed second theater introduced the company's signature look.

•

(opposite)

Ushers are briefed before a performance.

theater opened on schedule on July 2 with a comeback performance of *Madame Butterfly*. Later that summer, when flames flickered and smoke billowed from the stage during Henze's *The Bassarids*, it was all just part of the show. The new theater quickly became the company's bold new signature, with its two giant sweeping roofs arching toward each other in a classic tango embrace but not quite meeting—a twenty-two-foot gap leaving the middle portion of the auditorium open to the sky, the stars—and the rain.

There had been talk about the need to cover the entire theater since the first season, a summer of unprecedented storms that forced the postponement of several performances. Over the years, there had been several occasions when audience members got soaked as cold rain poured into the house, while on stage the singers kept going, sometimes inaudibly, braving wind, thunder, or a roaring downpour. In 1963, a retractable roof was proposed to protect audiences from passing storms, but the idea was dropped. Taking in opera under the stars had become part of the Santa Fe allure, and over the years audiences gladly took their chances with northern New Mexico's quick-changing weather for the heady experience of opera *al fresco*. Technically, only

John Crosby rehearses
in the second theater.

Sitzprobe for *The English Cat*, 1985.

Music Director Alan Gilbert
rehearses the orchestra.

534 seats were open to the elements, and statistics showed that on average only four performances were dampened by rain each summer.

Then came 1991. It rained during twenty-two of the season's thirty-seven performances, from short passing showers to all-night soakers; the gift shop sold out its 1,200 ponchos by mid-July and had to order another 1,000. It was by far the worst summer weather Crosby could remember, and he finally decided it was time to do something. In 1994, The Santa Fe Opera announced plans to cover the entire auditorium and to increase the theater capacity to 2,234, which was still significantly smaller than most American opera houses and in keeping with the intimacy of the European theaters that Crosby admired. The design was entrusted to the high-profile New York firm of Polshek and Partners, which was responsible for the successful, much-publicized renovation of Carnegie Hall. The firm would later gain further attention for the Rose Center at Manhattan's American Museum of Natural History, with its theatrical globe-in-a-glass-box, and for the William J. Clinton presidential library in Little Rock, Arkansas.

Less than twenty-four hours after the last performance of the 1997 season, *La traviata*, the 1,889 seats in the opera's theater were torn out. Work continued throughout the winter, and even though December snowstorms in southern New Mexico delayed delivery of steel from San Angelo, Texas, the new theater was completed on schedule. Board president Nancy Zeckendorf was a major force in the success of the capital campaign. Under her leadership, $20.5 million—the entire cost of the building—was raised. The Santa Fe Opera unveiled its third house on July 3, 1998, with a performance of *Madame Butterfly*, forty-one years to the day after the company burst on the scene with its very first *Butterfly*.

In order to "preserve memories of earlier opera theaters on the site," James Stewart Polshek wanted to build the new house on the existing footprint, anchored by four massive concrete columns that marked the corners of the original stage. Essentially, he hung an entirely new structure on an old skeleton, still maintaining Santa Fe's signature silhouette, with its two floating roofs now linked in one grand,

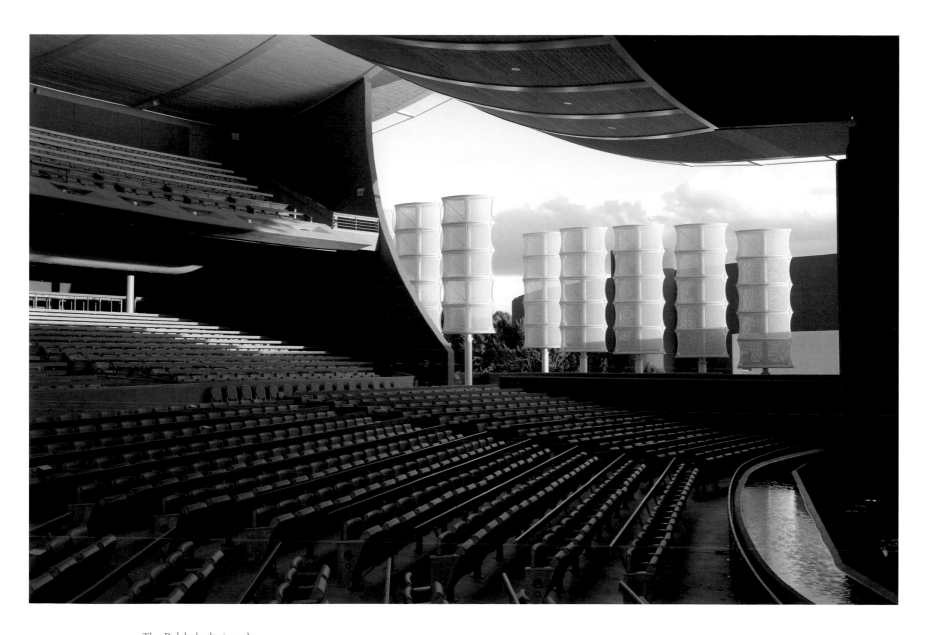

The Polshek-designed
third theater, 1998.

Production Director Paul Horpedahl
and General Director Richard Gaddes
watch a technical rehearsal.

On stage during a rehearsal
for *Peter Grimes*, 2005.

BACKSTAGE ARTISANS CREATE ONSTAGE MAGIC.

Painting scenery on
the back deck, 1984.

umbrella-like sweep. A system of eight steel masts and twenty-six tension rods—the theater's spindly new spine, blinding white against the blue of the sky—elegantly carries the roof's dead load of 435 tons onto the old columns. Jack Purcell, whose rifle had helped site the original house and who had overseen the acoustical design of the 1967 theater, was consulted once again to supervise the curvature of the new ceiling, which carries the burden of acoustics in a theater without walls.

Fittingly, the opera house is a highly dramatic building. The dialogue between the architecture and the setting links "performer and patron to land and sky," in Polshek's words, and the contrast of a stunningly new building on an ancient site suggests "permanence and change, stability and mobility, memory and aspirations"—qualities that continue to inform the work of the company itself. The new theater, like the previous ones that stood on the same place, ignores the familiar sensations that cultural buildings have given us over the centuries—secure enclosure, a safe vault of artistic treasures—in favor of openness and freedom, and a certain informality that is, at first, so unexpected in an opera house. This is very much an opera theater for the twenty-first century, down to the electronic titles on the back of each seat. Technicians from Santa Fe and the Met sketched out the original idea on bar napkins at a local watering hole. The system made its Santa Fe debut in 1999, and the company is the first in the country to provide titles in Spanish as well as in English.

The Santa Fe stage is distinctive, not only because it has no back wall, but also because it lacks a curtain and flies, which means that all scene changes take place in full view of the audience. An open-air stage provides unique challenges, from blowing rain to sudden wind gusts, a nagging problem since the first season. Eight slim white baffles that stand along the south side of the theater like giant Noguchi paper lanterns help cut the wind in the auditorium itself. It can be a tough theater for designers, who are used to working with a conventional proscenium, and it also creates a very tight summer schedule, since all lighting and dress rehearsals have to be held at night on nonperformance dates. But it also makes for an operagoing experience of unusual intimacy and visual drama.

This is a setting worthy of opera, and Santa Fe directors regularly use the surrounding mountains, the great expanse of darkening sky, or the moonlit hills to evoke an opera's time and place—most famously in *Madame Butterfly,* when the shimmering lights of Los Alamos, twenty miles away in the foothills of the Jemez, suggest Puccini's Nagasaki, ironically one of the towns nearly destroyed by the atomic bomb developed on that very mesa. Occasionally, the stage picture even

Constructing the set for
Peter Grimes, 2005.

spills over onto the adjacent landscape, un-expectedly blurring the line between real-ity and make-believe—the dazzling Fourth of July fireworks display that lit up the hills at the opening of *The Mother of Us All*, or the flares set out on the piñon-dotted ridges behind the open stage to launch the Dionysian rites of *The Bassarids*.

Nature sometimes adds its own effects on cue, setting off giant zigzags of lightning perfectly timed to accompany Don Giovanni's descent into hell, or unleashing a torren-tial downpour during the opening storm at sea of *The Flying Dutchman*. Once, during the run of Cavalli's *La Calisto*, a full lunar eclipse competed with the huge man-made moon ris-ing at the back of the stage. Composer John Eaton was sitting in the theater one night when rain and wind suddenly blew up, reminding him of the opening storm of *The Tempest*, his favorite Shakespeare play since childhood, which he decided on the spot to use as the subject for the opera he had been commissioned to write for Santa Fe. Nature came full circle: at the 1985 premiere, distant, menacing thunder accompa-nied Eaton's *The Tempest*.

Unlike most opera companies, The Santa Fe Opera owns its entire facility from top to bottom. As a result, running an opera house is more complicated in Santa Fe, and Gaddes

Apprentices leaving a
rehearsal hall at the Ranch.

often has said that his job is like running a combination of Disneyland and a holiday resort—one minute he's negotiating long-distance with a singer's agent and the next he's supervising the paving of a road. Backstage is a world unto itself—four floors descending from stage-level dressing rooms to subterranean vaults where old productions, shelves upon shelves of props, and thousands of costumes sit in storage. On the floors between are the shops—the costume shop, which has grown from a modest enterprise with five home sewing machines to a bustling, high-tech workplace of more than seventy stitchers and tailors; the props department, with a huge inventory of items from hat pins and demitasse spoons to columns, baroque mirrors, towering trees, and even stone statuary from the 1957 *Butterfly*; and the scenery shop, a Nibelheim-like place of welding sparks and persistent ham-mering, which builds nearly all the company's sets, in order to accommodate the unusual requirements of the stage.

The Santa Fe season lasts just two months, but produc-tion is a year-round activity: the first preliminary designs for the next year normally arrive at the end of June, the same week the current season opens. Working drawings are pre-pared in September, while that summer's season is put to bed, and construction of sets and costumes begins on-site later in the autumn. In the winter, the company starts assembling

Rehearsal of *The Devils of Loudon*
at O'Shaughnessy Hall, 1969.

Stage director Jonathan Miller
holds a master class, 1999.

LONGTIME EMPLOYEES
WITH RICHARD GADDES
Tom Morris, 28 years
Ben Saiz, 41 years
Brad Woolbright, 29 years
Jeanne Boyles, 22 years

its summer crew, which blossoms from fifteen full-timers to nearly two hundred, including some seventy apprentices. By mid-February, the first of the summer people show up—scenic artists, members of the props crew. The rest come in waves throughout the late spring; by the beginning of June, backstage at The Santa Fe Opera is at capacity.

Over the years, the quaint old San Juan Ranch has been transformed into a state-of-the-art facility. Much of the original land, once covered with little but piñon and tumbleweed, has been planted with crested wheat and buffalo grasses, Russian olive trees, lilacs, apricots, rosebushes, and towering Siberian elms; in 1994 a wetlands system was designed to recycle wastewater from toilets and sinks for irrigating the site. A cluster of simple rehearsal pavilions was built downhill from the Ranch house after the fire. On a typical summer afternoon, simultaneous rehearsals for three or four productions regularly fill the air with song. Up on the hill next to the theater stands Stieren Orchestra Hall, built in 2000 and named for Jane and Arthur Stieren, who often have contributed to the Opera's wish list over the years. A long-needed space for orchestra and staging rehearsals, Stieren replicates the size and configuration of the theater stage, with a floor seventy feet wide and seventy feet deep and a mammoth sliding glass wall that opens to the mountains out back.

The original ranch house is now the administration building; guest rooms have become offices—they still open directly onto the portal—and new wings have been added as the staff has grown. The lounge, with its high, beamed ceiling and central fireplace, is booked up with lessons, coaching sessions, and ensemble rehearsals. Staff members still fix their lunches in the old kitchen, with its linoleum counter tops and original butcher-block island, but the days when the entire company might dine together on steaks cooked in the outdoor fireplace, sitting at tables scattered on the portal, are long gone. Today the dining room itself hosts more meetings than meals. The Great Lawn, where *Madame Butterfly* was rehearsed the first summer, is regularly crisscrossed by singers with cell phones to their ears—ring tones from *Carmen* and *The Magic Flute* now compete with the sound of sopranos and baritones at work in modern-day Santa Fe.

In late afternoon, an acrobat
practices against the
backdrop of the Sangre
de Cristo Mountains.

Stieren Orchestra Hall
exterior (above) and
interior (right) with artist
Gronk preparing his
set for *Ainadamar*, 2005.

Two views of the deck
behind the theater.

ELEKTRA
Richard Strauss
2000

Mary Jane Johnson

CHAMPIONING

STRAUSS

SALOME
Richard Strauss
1978

Josephine Barstow
Ragnar Ulfung

Richard Strauss had been dead just eight years when The Santa Fe Opera opened. But to the music-loving public, he was a distant figure—a famous name from another era. Unlike Stravinsky, his colleague of a good half century—only eighteen years his junior, yet of a completely different musical generation—Strauss had not stayed in the public eye, and during the last decades of his life he had watched his career fade. Once the richest and most famous composer alive, he had outlived his popularity. At the time of his death, Strauss was known for just a handful of the high-octane orchestral tone poems he wrote at the end of the nineteenth century and for three operas he composed early in the twentieth century, all signposts of the modern age—*Salome,* his shocking adaptation of a play by Oscar Wilde; *Elektra,* which bordered on the avant-garde; and *Der Rosenkavalier,* which confounded the critics with its pretty waltzes and then turned out to be the biggest success of all.

When Crosby started studying music, his teachers—including one who had known Strauss personally—told him that the great Bavarian composer had nothing to say after *Der Rosenkavalier.* This was the standard view at the time, and Strauss's late works, almost without exception, were dismissed as passé. Crosby himself was more impressed by Strauss's early orchestral music—a radio broadcast of the

tone poem *Don Juan* had made him an overnight fan—and he wasn't particularly interested in any of Strauss's operas. Later on, he couldn't even remember whether it was *Salome* or *Rosenkavalier* that he heard first.

But when Crosby helped to prepare a workshop production of Strauss's *Daphne* in the early fifties, he realized that he had been missing something extraordinary. Then, after seeing a captivating performance of *Capriccio* in Europe in 1952, Crosby was convinced that Strauss needed a serious reevaluation and that his operas deserved to be heard. In the fifties, more than half of Strauss's fifteen operas were all but unknown, and six of them had never even been staged in the United States. The Santa Fe Opera would change that.

Santa Fe started in 1958 with *Capriccio,* Strauss's farewell to opera, and the music world immediately took notice of this year-old company, which was presenting the American premiere of Strauss's swan song just sixteen years after the composer himself had led the premiere in Munich. *Capriccio* is an opera *about* opera, with the apt subtitle "a conversation piece for music," and today it is widely recognized as one of Strauss's finest works, capped by a soprano soliloquy that is a highpoint of the literature. Although *Capriccio* was slow to catch on in this country, today it is considered prime

DAPHNE
Richard Strauss
1996

Janice Watson

CAPRICCIO
Richard Strauss
1993

Sheri Greenawald
Richard Stilwell

CAPRICCIO
Richard Strauss
1993

Molly Rose

Strauss, and Santa Fe played a major role in its reappraisal.

In 1964, the centenary of Strauss's birth, The Santa Fe Opera gave the American premiere of *Daphne,* the work that is said to have ushered in the Indian summer of Strauss's old age, with Sylvia Stahlman in the title role and Vera Zorina making her debut as a stage director. *Daphne* occupies a special place in the Strauss output. It is nearly impossible to stage sensibly—the heroine, a mythical brokenhearted nymph, is turned into a laurel tree at the end—yet it contains some of the composer's most glorious music. Strauss himself, in his final years, played the luminous final scene over and over at the piano. (More than half a century later, Osvaldo Golijov listened to Strauss's finale repeatedly as he composed *Ainadamar,* which Santa Fe performed in 2005.) Santa Fe turned out to be the perfect setting for *Daphne,* an opera that takes place in the mountains and asks for Apollo's entrance to be accompanied by thunder and lightning, an effect New Mexico's skies provided on more than one occasion. When it began to rain at the end of the opening night performance, Stahlman, singing on the open stage, magically appeared to

DIE SCHWEIGSAME FRAU
Richard Strauss
1991

Brenda Harris
Donald Wages
Erie Mills
Eric Halfvarson
Mark Thomsen

•

(*opposite*)

DIE LIEBE DER DANAE
Richard Strauss
1982

Ashley Putnam
Victor Braun

have tears streaming down her face. For many years, Santa Fe remained the only American company with *Daphne* in its repertory. (The New York stage premiere wasn't given until 2004.) Santa Fe revived *Daphne* in 1981 with Roberta Alexander and in 1996 with Janice Watson—making something of a house specialty of a work that was largely ignored elsewhere.

With Santa Fe's 1982 staging of the obscure *Die Liebe der Danae,* the company demonstrated the depth of its commitment to Strauss's operatic output. "If there is now a growing audience in this country that is receptive not only to the earlier works of Richard Strauss . . . but also to the once-scorned products of his later years, John Crosby and his Santa Fe Opera may take some of the credit," *The New York Times* wrote that summer. The next-to-last opera to come from Strauss's pen, *Die Liebe der Danae* is the only one that he never saw. It was composed at the height of World War II, and after Hitler's declaration of "total war" in August 1944, the world premiere that was scheduled for that summer's Salzburg Festival turned into a private dress rehearsal. This "cheerful mythology" wasn't publicly performed until 1952, three years after the

ARIADNE AUF NAXOS
Richard Strauss
1990

Alessandra Marc
Ben Heppner

ARIADNE AUF NAXOS
Richard Strauss
1999

Wilbur Pauley
Erie Mills
Keith Jameson
Gert Henning-Jensen

INTERMEZZO
Richard Strauss
1994

Sheri Greenawald
Erie Mills
Sara Seglem

composer's death. There had been only a handful of subsequent productions, most of them in Munich, before Santa Fe took up the cause. The company's stagings—it revived the work in 1985, directed by Bruce Donnell in his Santa Fe debut—offered music lovers, Strauss fanatics, and envious critics their first look at what still remains a curiosity.

During the 1980s, Santa Fe completed its campaign to introduce the rest of Strauss's operatic output to this country. *Intermezzo,* the composer's semiautobiographical family portrait, had been ignored by American opera houses for sixty years when Santa Fe gave the U.S. premiere in 1984. Santa Fe was fortunate to have the distinguished Swedish soprano Elisabeth Söderström singing the role of Christine, loosely based on the composer's feisty wife Pauline. Alan Titus appeared as the composer, here called Robert Storch. The Metropolitan had produced *The Egyptian Helen,* arguably Strauss's least-known opera, a few months after the controversial Dresden premiere in 1928. But the work hadn't been seen on an American stage since then, and the version Santa Fe presented in 1986—a revision Strauss prepared in 1933—had never been performed in this country at all. The last of the six operas by Strauss that Santa Fe introduced was his antiwar statement *Friedenstag,* staged by the company

in 1988, just one day short of the fiftieth anniversary of the Munich premiere.

The Santa Fe Opera wrote itself into the history books with the American premieres of these six Strauss operas, but over the years it has hardly neglected the composer's other stage works, beginning with the first season's *Ariadne auf Naxos.* In fact, the company has produced more operas by Strauss than by any other composer. It has staged *Salome* as often as *Madame Butterfly* or *La bohème,* and it has produced *Der Rosenkavalier* five times, including the summer after the fire, when, in a frugal season, Strauss's most sumptuous opera was played against bare stage walls, with no more than a few pieces of furniture. (The casting, with Helen Vanni as the Marschallin and Judith Raskin as Sophie, was far from Spartan.) For the company's first *Elektra* in 1980, the young Swedish director Göran Järvefelt, a former assistant to Ingmar Bergman, made his American debut with one of Santa Fe's most powerful but controversial productions— a "sadomasochistic nightmare in black, white, and red," wrote the critic from the *Los Angeles Times.* With his next company assignment, the American premiere of *Intermezzo,* Järvefelt charmed audiences and critics alike with his fresh approach: "Santa Fe is different from European houses in that there are no clichés," he said.

INTERMEZZO
Richard Strauss
1984

John Stewart
Elisabeth Söderström

DER ROSENKAVALIER
Richard Strauss
1989

Sally Wolf
Cheryl Parrish
Jeanne Piland

After the presentation of *Friedenstag* in 1988, just two of Strauss's operas had gone unperformed in Santa Fe: his first, the Wagnerian *Guntram,* which is regularly deemed unstageworthy (it was a flop at the premiere and has rarely been seen since), and *Die Frau ohne Schatten,* which Crosby fully intended to produce, despite its demands for major voices in five tough and unforgiving roles, but gave up on more than once. Long after Strauss and Santa Fe had become nearly synonymous to the American opera public, Crosby insisted that the company never set out to produce all of Strauss's operas. Nevertheless, the only other company in the world that can rival Santa Fe's devotion is the venerable Bavarian State Opera in Munich, Strauss's hometown. Even the Salzburg Festival, which Strauss helped to found, did not always so boldly champion the works by the composer who lived ninety miles down the road in Garmisch.

More than once over the years, Crosby visited the Strauss villa in the Bavarian countryside, to study the composer's original manuscripts, to visit with Strauss's descendants, and to see where Strauss once lived and worked. He sat at the great oak desk, with its postcard view of the Alps, where Strauss composed all his scores beginning with *Elektra,* and the living room piano, where the composer would try out his new ideas on Pauline. Crosby had a steel-trap memory, and when he saw the designs for Santa Fe's 1984 production of *Intermezzo,* which is set in a villa plainly modeled after the Garmisch house, he quickly pointed out that the scale of the piano was all wrong. Strauss himself would have been astonished that it was a new opera house in the American Southwest, not one of our old-line companies, that introduced six of his works to this country.

Strauss's grandson Christian came to Santa Fe several times, most recently in 1996, to see for himself how the Opera was honoring the great German composer. Among Crosby's most treasured possessions were some manuscript pages for *Capriccio* that Christian and the composer's daughter-in-law Alice gave him in recognition of all that he and the Santa Fe company had done for the reputation of Strauss's operas in America.

DER ROSENKAVALIER
Richard Strauss
1992

Ashley Putnam
Susanne Mentzer

A DREAM PLAY
Ingvar Lidholm
1998

Sylvia McNair

FIRST NIGHTS

The American premiere of Alban Berg's *Lulu* in Santa Fe on July 28, 1963, drew the largest crowd in the seven-year history of the company, "with standees all the way back to the parking lot," as *Time* reported. Crosby had seen Berg's landmark opera in Europe, and he was amazed that the work had never been performed in this country. He knew Santa Fe was the place to stage it, and he decided to make it the centerpiece of the company's 1963 season. Even though only two performances were scheduled, rehearsals stretched on for more than two months and tested The Santa Fe Opera's resources like nothing before. *Lulu* was a milestone for the young company, and more than one critic marveled that this historic premiere took place in Santa Fe, not at one of the country's big-city houses.

Lulu was Berg's final work—it consumed the last eight years of his life—and when he died of blood poisoning on Christmas Eve in 1935, he had completed the opera except for orchestrating parts of the third act. What Santa Fe presented in 1963, as did the Zurich Opera, which gave the world premiere in 1937, was a great, tantalizing torso: two complete acts plus fragments of a third. Helene Berg was highly protective of her husband's memory—she left their Vienna apartment untouched after his death, down to the unemptied ashtrays—and she was particularly sensitive about letting anyone finish orchestrating *Lulu*, a tale about the destructive power of erotic love that struck close to

LULU
Alban Berg
1963

Joan Carroll

home. (Helene had long suspected that her husband was having an affair.) Finally, Stravinsky, who considered Berg one of a handful of opera's "great progressivists," wrote Helene a letter on behalf of Crosby and proposed the idea of a private performance of Act 3 in Santa Fe as a kind of dry run. Helene agreed, as long as she was present to hear it for herself. But she quickly became finicky and demanding (she asked that a private jet fly her from Vienna to Santa Fe), and the entire plan soon fell through. Eventually, she refused to let anyone even see the manuscript of the opera, claiming that her husband's spirit regularly visited her and begged her to leave the work unfinished.

Helene Berg died in 1976, just six months before the Met was scheduled to present *Lulu* for the first time. Suddenly the race to finish the third act picked up, and the world's biggest opera companies, including the Met, were vying to give the premiere of the complete *Lulu,* with the nod eventually going to the Paris Opéra. When Crosby had first negotiated with Berg's Vienna publisher, Alfred Kalmus of Universal Editions, to present *Lulu* in 1963, they had agreed that Santa Fe would give the American premiere of Act 3 when it was finally released. Kalmus had since died, but Crosby collected all the memos, cables, and letters detailing the arrangements, and he managed to convince Universal to let Santa Fe present the complete *Lulu* for the first time in the United States, right after the Paris premiere.

LULU
Alban Berg
1963

George Shirley
Joan Carroll

On July 28, 1979, nearly forty-four years after Berg's death, *Lulu* was finally performed in its entirety in this country. Many of the critics who came to Santa Fe that week also had been in Paris for the world premiere of the complete *Lulu* in February, which, in Patrice Chéreau's controversial staging, took great liberties with Berg's explicit stage directions. The Santa Fe production was painstakingly prepared; during rehearsals, the cast screened Louise Brooks's Lulu in the 1928 silent film of Frank Wedekind's *Pandora's Box,* and Colin Graham's staging was "thoughtful, imaginative, and responsible—unlike the world premiere of the complete *Lulu* in Paris," as Andrew Porter wrote in *The New Yorker.* Nancy Shade was a mesmerizing, vocally magnificent Lulu, and Michael Tilson Thomas, in his company debut, led a powerful reading of Berg's richest and most challenging score. John Conklin's sets and costumes were based on the designs the late Rudolf Heinrich made for the 1963 Santa Fe production. *Lulu* was one of the company's most telling achievements—a night when it secured its bid to be ranked among opera's most influential houses. "The Santa Fe Opera, which has taken the lead on so many occasions since its inception in 1957," wrote *The New York Times,* "has once again demonstrated its enterprise, imagination, and importance to opera in America."

LULU
Alban Berg
Complete Version
1979

Lenus Carlson
Nancy Shade

Santa Fe's commitment to presenting new operas was cemented the very first summer with Marvin David Levy's *The Tower,* a comic opera about the marriage of King Solomon's daughter. "The measure of The Santa Fe Opera's enterprise is that in its first season it has produced a new American opera," *The New York Times* noted. For its second season, the company commissioned an opera from Carlisle Floyd, the composer of the classic American tragedy *Susannah.* But Floyd's *Wuthering Heights,* based on Emily Brontë's novel, was a disappointment, despite the passionate performance by Phyllis Curtin as Cathy.

In 1961, Santa Fe boasted the participation of the two men who were arguably the world's most famous living composers, Igor Stravinsky and the German-born Paul Hindemith, who both came to conduct their works. (Seeing the two men interact was like watching Mozart talking to Bach, a singer said that summer.) By 1961, Stravinsky was part of the Santa Fe family, but Hindemith, an American citizen since 1946, had been to New Mexico only once before on vacation, and he was new to the company. Having grown up in a country where people took their music seriously—"Opera is established over in Europe," he said at a press conference held at the Ranch, "wherever you go, there is an opera house"—he immediately recognized the significance of this young American venture.

LULU
Alban Berg
1979

William Dooley
Nancy Shade
Barry Busse
Claudia Catania

Hindemith's 1929 operatic satire, *News of the Day,* had been performed throughout Europe, but never before in this country. A cautionary tale about privacy and publicity, *News of the Day* had made headlines of its own when Hitler walked out of a performance in Berlin, incensed by the sight of a soprano singing from her bathtub, even though she was merely extolling the joys of hot running water. The Santa Fe production was updated to include references to TV and space travel, but Hindemith pointed out that the issue wasn't modernity: "Is it genuine or not? Is it convincing? That is the question that should be asked," he said at the Santa Fe press conference. In Santa Fe, where going to an opera was still something of a novelty, the answer was a resounding yes. (Santa Fe revived *News of the Day* in 1981 in a staging by Lou Galterio.) In 1967, after Hindemith's death, The Santa Fe Opera gave the American premiere of his first opera, *Cardillac,* only hours before fire broke out in the theater.

During the 1965 season, The Santa Fe Opera gave the American premiere of *The Stag King* by the thirty-nine-year-old German composer Hans Werner Henze. It was the beginning of a thirty-five-year relationship that would result in the American premieres of six of Henze's operas. A remarkably gifted and prolific composer, Henze has concentrated on opera to a degree that is unusual in the post–World War II era,

NEWS OF THE DAY
Paul Hindemith
1981

Jean Kraft
Mary Shearer
James Atherton

and Santa Fe turned out to be an ideal theater to introduce his works, beginning with its magical production of *The Stag King,* which featured children costumed as animals and choristers as trees and was capped by fireworks that lit up the night sky.

Henze came to Santa Fe himself two years later to supervise *Boulevard Solitude,* the opera that first brought his name to the public's attention in the early fifties. A retelling of the story of Manon Lescaut updated to Paris after the Second World War, the opera opened in Santa Fe just seven days after the theater burned to the ground, with an improvised set and modern-dress costumes culled from local closets. Every seat in Sweeney Gymnasium was filled, and the audience roared its approval. Henze was back in town the following summer to conduct *The Bassarids* in the new house. Based on Euripides and with a libretto by W. H. Auden and Chester Kallman, the team responsible for *The Rake's Progress, The Bassarids* often has been called Henze's greatest opera. It had previously been undertaken only in Salzburg, Berlin, and Milan, at La Scala. The Santa Fe production, conducted by the composer and directed by Bodo Igesz, with a cast featuring John Reardon, was a triumph. But it also put a temporary end to Santa Fe's Henze survey, because after composing *The Bassarids,* Henze announced that he had given up on opera—the score "seemed to exhaust the form of opera as I had looked at it."

VON HEUTE AUF MORGEN
Arnold Schoenberg
1980

Carol Wilcox
William Stone
Mary Shearer
Barry Busse

THE ITALIAN STRAW HAT
Nino Rota
1977

James Atherton
D'Artagnan Petty

Then, after a long sabbatical from the opera house, Henze returned to form with *We Come to the River,* which Santa Fe picked up and staged in 1984. A bloody antiwar statement—it begins in a slaughterhouse and ends in an asylum—*We Come to the River* called on the resources of the entire company; it demands more than one hundred singing roles and divides the stage into three separate areas (each with its own chamber orchestra), allowing two or more scenes to play simultaneously. Powerfully staged by Alfred Kirchner and authoritatively conducted by Dennis Russell Davies, *We Come to the River* was a dazzling confirmation of the company's daring and enterprise.

The following summer, Santa Fe presented Henze's newest opera, *The English Cat,* in a production by Charles Ludlum, the founder of New York's Ridiculous Theater Company, who had never staged an opera before (although he had presented a send-up of Wagner's *Ring* with lesbian motorcyclists as the Valkyries). Based on a tale by Honoré de Balzac, with a libretto by Edward Bond, the Santa Fe *English Cat* was the first production of Henze's comic parable to be sung in English, the language in which it was written. Ludlum created a delightfully fresh staging of Henze's anthropomorphic tale, which, in addition to a number of cats, features birds, a sheep, a trio of dogs, and an orphaned mouse named Louise. Henze came to Santa Fe to oversee the production—while he was in town he wrote a new orchestral interlude to cover a scene

change—and once again he was thrilled to see his work get the Santa Fe treatment: "There is a sense of dedication in the whole place, from the hatmakers to the coaches, from the leading soprano to the youngest apprentice," he said that summer. Henze also found Santa Fe an ideal place to compose, quieter even than his home in the Italian countryside (he finished his seventh symphony in Santa Fe in 1984 and worked on a cello concerto during the summer of *The English Cat*). Although Henze never returned to Santa Fe; in 2000 the company staged the American premiere of his newest operatic work, *Venus and Adonis,* a one-act Shakespearean ode for singers and dancers—a lovely footnote to the Opera's bold Henze chapter.

Over the years, Santa Fe has given American premieres of significant operas by some of the biggest names in modern music. Shostakovich's experimental early opera *The Nose,* based on Nikolay Gogol's absurdist tale about a petty bureaucrat who wakes up one morning to find his nose missing, received only its fourth staging in forty-five years. *Die Jakobsleiter,* a major if fragmentary work by Schoenberg (he worked on it intermittently throughout his life and never finished the score), was given its first American performances—and its first staging anywhere—in Santa Fe in 1968. Schoenberg's comedy of manners, *Von Heute auf Morgen,* was produced in Santa Fe in 1980—fifty years

THE ENGLISH CAT
Hans Werner Henze
1985

THE SORROWS OF YOUNG WERTHER
Hans-Jürgen von Bose
1992

Kurt Ollmann
Charlotte Hellekant

VENUS AND ADONIS
Hans Werner Henze
2000

Lauren Flanigan
Stephen West
Sarita Allen

after it was first performed in Frankfurt—
as part of a groundbreaking Schoenberg
triple bill, along with *Erwartung* and *Die
Jakobsleiter.* When Santa Fe jumped on
the Benjamin Britten bandwagon in 1973,
it was with the American premiere of
his brand-new *Owen Wingrave,* originally
written for television and recently staged at Covent Garden.
The Cunning Little Vixen was almost unknown when Santa
Fe presented Colin Graham's production of Janáček's opera
in 1975, some three decades after its Czech premiere. Santa
Fe's outdoor theater provided an ideal setting for the opera's
dialogue between man and nature—the cast includes a
mosquito, a cricket, a grasshopper, and dancing hedgehogs.
Today, Janáček is recognized as one of modern music's greatest pioneers, and *Vixen* is considered one of his most important works.

Santa Fe has played a key role in renewing interest in
several early-twentieth-century composers. The American
premiere of Alexander Zemlinsky's *A Florentine Tragedy* in
Santa Fe in 1984 came very early in the revival of this long-
neglected Viennese composer, who was both a friend of
Mahler and Schoenberg's brother-in-law. Santa Fe's provoca-
tive production was not universally admired, and one opera-
goer, irate over the heroine's disrobing—even though it was
far upstage and dimly lit—filed a complaint with the sheriff's
office. In 1993, Santa Fe introduced American audiences to

THE NOSE
Dmitri Shostakovich
1987

James Ramlet
Alan Titus

The Protagonist and *The Tsar Has His Pho-
tograph Taken,* two works that Kurt Weill
composed before *The Threepenny Opera,*
some sixty-five years after they were first
staged in Germany.

Even legendary New Mexico recluse
Georgia O'Keeffe showed up for the world
premiere of Heitor Villa-Lobos's *Yerma* in 1971—curious,
no doubt, to see the scenic designs by Giorgio de Chirico,
the Italian modernist painter. (Simply attired as always,
O'Keeffe wore a plain black gown and white rebozo, her
silver hair in a topknot.) Villa-Lobos had finished his only
opera in 1955, but he died in 1959 before he could get it
produced, and negotiations over the rights were tied up in
litigation for a decade. With a libretto based almost word
for word on Federico García Lorca's play, *Yerma* achieves the
summation of Villa-Lobos's eclectic style. To prepare for her
role as Yerma, Mirna Lacambra went to Granada, where she
spent Easter Sunday with García Lorca's family, including his
brother Francisco and his sister Isabel. Four abstract paintings
by de Chirico—"landscapes" characteristic of the master in
their haunting mystery and starkness—were projected on
the walls of a simple set designed by Allen Charles Klein. Sixteen years after the opera was finished, *Yerma* finally received
its world premiere in the original Spanish in Santa Fe, with
a cast including a young Frederica von Stade. Señora Villa-
Lobos, the composer's widow, came from her home in Rio

THE CUNNING
LITTLE VIXEN
Leoš Janáček
1975

Barbara Hendricks
Vinson Cole

YERMA
Heitor Villa-Lobos
1971

Theodor Uppman

de Janeiro to attend the opening, which was greeted with a standing ovation.

Of all the operas Santa Fe has premiered, none made bigger headlines than *Opera* by the Italian avant-garde composer Luciano Berio, which was commissioned by the company for the 1970 season. At the work's end, there were cheers and rhythmic clapping, but there was also an outburst, rowdy even by operatic standards, of catcalls and boos and a shower of program books tossed into the air. *Opera* was Berio's first large-scale work for the stage, and it bravely questioned the conventions that have governed opera for four centuries. In his densely layered, dreamlike score, Berio weaves together a staggering array of ideas—from references to Monteverdi's *Orfeo* (history's first major opera, as old as Santa Fe) and the sinking of the *Titanic* (a recurring symbol for the decline of opera itself) to shock effects, including strobe lights, nudity, and a nightmare sequence of screaming children. Santa Fe's orchestra and a large cast of singers, led by the redoubtable Dennis Russell Davies, in his company debut, were fully up to the challenges posed by a kind of music that was new, even foreign, to most of them.

The critics—and there were plenty in the house—were baffled or guarded in their praise, although a few recognized this as a bold new kind of theatrical art form. If *Opera* was a flop, as many thought at the time, it was the kind of failure that any adventuresome opera company would be proud to claim, for it broke new ground, tested the limits of the art form with intelligence and wit, and made people think. No one took *Opera* lightly (one critic suggested that a company capable of commissioning such a work should go out of business), and once again the opera house was the place of controversy, heated debate, and volatile audience reaction that it had regularly been in the eighteenth and nineteenth centuries.

In 1994, The Santa Fe Opera announced that it had commissioned three American composers to write their first operas. The first of the commissions, *Modern Painters*, by David Lang, a Henze protégé and one of the few composers of his young generation to write a traditional opera, is based on the life and works of the uncompromising English art critic John Ruskin, who surely would not have known what to think of Lang's hip and irreverent music.

The second Santa Fe commission went to Tobias Picker, who had been looking for an opera subject for eight years when he came across a television documentary about the young New England mill worker Emmeline Mosher, a single mother who was forced to give up her baby son and then unknowingly married him twenty years later. Picker knew at once that he had found his story. With his strong, emotionally direct music and a dark, spare production that stunningly evoked the plain mill-town setting, *Emmeline* was a triumph for Santa Fe. An American opera with an all-American cast,

YERMA
Heitor Villa-Lobos
1971

Mirna Lacambra

THE DEVILS OF LOUDON
Krzysztof Penderecki
1969

Richard Cross
John Reardon

OPERA
Luciano Berio
1970

Richard Lombardi

EMMELINE
Tobias Picker
1996

Patricia Racette
Anne-Marie Owens

EMMELINE
Tobias Picker
1996

Patricia Racette (far right)

Emmeline featured a career-defining performance of the opera's richly developed central role by Patricia Racette, herself a native New Englander. The Santa Fe production, directed by Francesca Zambello and conducted by George Manahan, was taped live for television and broadcast the following spring on PBS's *Great Performances*.

The third opera in the series was *Ashoka's Dream* by Peter Lieberson, who had spent his teenage summers roaming the Ranch and later working in the maintenance department when his mother, Vera Zorina, appeared with the company. Later, when Peter decided he wanted to be a composer, he went to see Stravinsky, a longtime family friend, to give him the news. "It is not enough to want," the maestro warned him. "You must *be*." By 1997, however, Lieberson had established himself as one of the rising stars among American composers, and *Ashoka's Dream* was not only a work of genuine originality but also one that brought the company full circle to the days when Zorina and the Stravinskys were members of the Opera family.

Beginning with Stravinsky and continuing with Hindemith and Henze, Santa Fe has drawn many composers from around the world to New Mexico to help introduce their works to America. Gian Carlo Menotti came to Santa Fe for the first U.S. staging of his opera "for children and

MODERN PAINTERS
David Lang
1995

François Le Roux
Sheila Nadler
Dale Travis
Judith Christin
John Joseph Concepcion
Ann Panagulias

those who like children," *Help, Help, The Globolinks!*, which featured the young company apprentice Judith Blegen not only singing but also playing the violin onstage (she studied both at the Curtis Institute of Music). Nino Rota failed to show up at the 1974 Academy Awards to pick up his Oscar for scoring *The Godfather, Part II*, but he came all the way from Italy in 1977 to see the American premiere of *The Italian Straw Hat*, his twenty-year-old featherweight transformation of Eugène Labiche's popular French farce—and rewrote the clarinet part during intermission.

The avant-garde Polish composer Krzysztof Penderecki was at the height of his notoriety when he came to Santa Fe in 1969 to oversee the preparation of his first opera, *The Devils of Loudon*, which had premiered in Hamburg the year before. That production was only a mixed success, and Penderecki was rewriting portions of the score throughout his stay in Santa Fe, right up to the last day of rehearsal. In Santa Fe, *The Devils of Loudon* was a hit, although some first nighters were put off by a graphic enema scene and simulated nudity, and Penderecki was thrilled that his idiosyncratic work had found an audience. Nearly twenty years later, he returned to Santa Fe for the first American performances of *The Black Mask*. "It is a very important place to be," Penderecki said, noting that Santa Fe was following only Salzburg and Vienna in staging the opera.

ASHOKA'S DREAM
Peter Lieberson
1997

Beau Palmer
Kurt Ollmann
John Atkins

A DREAM PLAY
Ingvar Lidholm
1998

Sylvia McNair
Thomas Barrett

MADAME MAO
Bright Sheng
2003

Mark Duffin
Robynne Redmon
Kelly Kaduce

133

Kaija Saariaho was a name hardly known to American audiences when she came to Santa Fe in 2002 for the U.S. premiere of her first opera, *L'amour de loin*, the tale of a twelfth-century troubadour who falls in love, sight unseen, with a woman who lives across the sea. Presented in cooperation with the Salzburg Festival and with the Théâtre du Châtelet in Paris, *L'amour de loin* was an international sensation. The Santa Fe production, staged by Peter Sellars in his company debut, set this minimalist drama on a bare stage flooded with water. The two lovers sang from narrow, eerily lit towers on opposite sides of the stage, which made the distance between them, physically and emotionally, hauntingly real. Only in the tragic finale were they brought together across the shimmering waters by a simple boat that glowed in the dark. Conducted by Robert Spano, the Santa Fe production was dominated by the definitive performance of Dawn Upshaw, returning to the company for the

L'AMOUR DE LOIN
Kaija Saariaho
2002

Monica Groop
Dawn Upshaw

first time in nearly a decade in a role that was written especially for her. *L'amour de loin* turned out to be the season's hottest ticket, and Gaddes opened the final dress rehearsal to a paying crowd in order to meet the demand.

With its 2003 production of Bright Sheng's powerful *Madame Mao*, an account of Jiang Ching's life told in flashback from the moment of her death, The Santa Fe Opera had presented forty American premieres and nine world premieres. Forty-nine premieres in about as many years is a yardstick few opera companies can hope to match. Not all of these forty-nine nights count among Santa Fe's finest, and not all of these operas will find a permanent home in the repertory. But it is a risk Santa Fe has chosen to take again and again. The company's track record for introducing neglected works by major composers and for taking chances on promising new scores demonstrates how much a single house can do to keep opera alive.

134

L'AMOUR DE LOIN
Kaija Saariaho
2002

Gerald Finley
Dawn Upshaw
Monica Groop

LUCIO SILLA
Wolfgang Amadeus Mozart
2005
Celena Shafer

DEBUTS AND
DISCOVERIES

Singers are drawn to The Santa Fe Opera, despite the altitude—at 7,500 feet, more than a mile higher than Salzburg, the air is thin enough to warrant keeping oxygen tanks backstage. The humidity on a typical July evening is a meager 28 percent, approaching Sahara levels. From the beginning, The Santa Fe Opera was a singer's company, but not in the traditional sense. One day in the mid-1950s, Jeannette Scovotti, a soprano who later sang Lucia in Santa Fe, told Crosby she was lucky to get a job on the boardwalk in Coney Island during the summer to pay for voice lessons. That got him thinking that Americans chased their best singers off to Europe at the end of the traditional opera season. What The Santa Fe Opera would provide was a place for young singers to get their first onstage experience, for promising young stars to tackle major roles, and for established artists to break in a new part, try something out-of-the-way, or simply recharge their batteries away from the hubbub of the international music scene. Almost at once, this changed the itinerary of American opera singers.

Growing up in Roswell, New Mexico, Susan Graham had her sights set on The Santa Fe Opera from an early age. For a girl whose ancestors helped tame the Southwest

COSÌ FAN TUTTE
Wolfgang Amadeus Mozart
1990

Susan Graham

•

(opposite)

LA BELLE HÉLÈNE
Jacques Offenbach
2003

Susan Graham
William Burden

(her grandfather rode out on a Conestoga wagon as a little boy), with cowboys and ranchers on both sides of the family, it was natural for her to want to sing at home. But when Graham auditioned for The Santa Fe apprentice program in the mid-1980s, she was young and green and didn't get past the preliminary round. It was only in 1989, after studying at the Manhattan School of Music and winning the Metropolitan Opera auditions, that she was invited to Santa Fe, as the understudy for Frederica von Stade in Massenet's *Chérubin* and to appear as Flora, a tiny role in *La traviata*. (Although she never did go on for von Stade, the celebrated mezzo became an important mentor for Graham, and they remain close friends.)

Since then, The Santa Fe Opera has hosted some of Graham's most important nights in an opera house. She tried out three of her signature roles in Santa Fe: Dorabella in *Così fan tutte* and the Composer in Strauss's *Ariadne auf Naxos* in 1990, and, on a now-famous night in 1991, her first Cherubino, opposite Bryn Terfel's first Figaro, in *The Marriage of Figaro*. Then, after spending several summers in Salzburg, where she developed something of a cult following, in 1998 she returned to Santa Fe a major star, to sing Berlioz's Beatrice,

THE STAG KING
Hans Werner Henze
1965

George Shirley

•

(opposite)
DON GIOVANNI
Wolfgang Amadeus Mozart
1972

Frederica von Stade
Michael Devlin

followed by Offenbach's Hélène and Cecilio in Mozart's *Lucio Silla*. Graham has come to think of The Santa Fe Opera as home, a place full of memories and familiar sensations—with the first gulp of air you inhale to sing "Voi che sapete," she once said, you know you're back in New Mexico.

Frederica von Stade was herself a little-known singer that summer in 1971 when she sang Cherubino in *Figaro* and appeared in the American premiere of Villa-Lobos's *Yerma*. After Cherubino in Santa Fe, she triumphed in the role in Paris—her European debut, under Sir Georg Solti—as well as at Glyndebourne and Salzburg. In 1972, she sang Zerlina for the first time in Santa Fe (it quickly became one of her signature parts) and her first Mélisande, an unconventional choice for a mezzo-soprano, but a role that she later repeated to great acclaim and recorded under Herbert von Karajan. She was an international star when she returned to Santa Fe a decade later for Ambroise Thomas's *Mignon*, a French Romantic rarity mounted just for her, and then in 1989 as Massenet's *Chérubin*, which picks up the story of Cherubino where Mozart leaves off—bringing von Stade back to the character with which she first charmed Santa Fe audiences. Von Stade continued to break new ground in Santa Fe,

taking on Handel's Xerxes for the company in 1993.

Many singers have come to think of Santa Fe as a place where they do their best work, and they return season after season. Santa Fe has long been the most casual and friendly of the big-league festivals. From the very beginning, it had a reputation as a place where singers had a good time as well as a great musical experience—a kind of summer camp in a picture-postcard setting. (Still, it must have come as something of a surprise to the singer in the early years who requested a room with an ocean view.) The environment is still refreshingly low-key and supportive, and singers regularly show up in the audience on their nights off to watch their colleagues at work. Every day between rehearsals, singers, designers, makeup artists, conductors, pianists—performers and behind-the-scenes people alike—gather in the poolside Cantina (Santa Fe's company cafeteria), lunching, nursing soft drinks, and talking shop, while spouses and children join in or take a dip in the pool.

In the early days, certain artists were not only in residence nearly every season, but they often sang several roles

140

THE ELIXIR OF LOVE
Gaetano Donizetti
1968

Gimi Beni

each summer—mezzo-soprano Elaine Bonazzi, who performed in Santa Fe for many years beginning in 1958, appeared in five different operas in 1963 alone, including the company's historic *Lulu,* and she even took on three separate parts in Ravel's *L'enfant et les sortilèges.* (Stravinsky said that her Baba the Turk in his *Rake's Progress* uncovered such tragic dimensions that it made him cry.) The Santa Fe Opera owes much of its identity to its regulars—singers such as Met favorite Helen Vanni, who joined the Santa Fe company for its second season, was its Cherubino of choice for many years, its Suzuki in three *Butterfly* productions, and Jocasta in *Oedipus rex* for Stravinsky; Gimi Beni, who appeared with the company off and on for more than thirty years; Judith Christin, who marked her nineteenth season in Santa Fe in 2005; Jean Kraft, who performed almost annually from the mid-sixties to the mid-eighties, often in several roles each summer; and Sheri Greenawald, who was a familiar Santa Fe presence for more than twenty years beginning in 1976, when she sang Mozart's Susanna, later moving on to the Countess in the same opera.

An opera company isn't like a ballet troupe or an orchestra, with a core of performers who appear night after night, season after season. Still, The Santa Fe Opera always has inspired uncommon devotion and loyalty, and it is not

unusual for a singer to spend the better part of a career in Santa Fe, appearing regularly or coming back every few years to try new parts. Andrew Foldi, who sang Doctor Bartolo in the first summer's *Barber of Seville,* gave his farewell performance as the Speaker in *The Magic Flute* nearly a quarter of a century later. Nico Castel, whose Santa Fe career ranged from Fenton in the 1958 *Falstaff* to Don Curzio in *Figaro* nearly thirty years later, now returns to work with company apprentices. Richard Stilwell, who first appeared in Santa Fe in 1971 and sang Pelléas opposite von Stade the next season, most recently sang with the company as the Music Master in *Ariadne auf Naxos* in 1999. Mary Jane Johnson, who made her company debut as Rosalinde in *Die Fledermaus* in 1982, later sang Mozart's Countess and Minnie in Puccini's *La fanciulla del West.* She also starred as Elektra in John Crosby's farewell performances of Strauss's opera before appearing as the scene-stealing Berta in *The Barber of Seville* in 2005. Over the years, many others have become family members—Kevin Langan, from the Opera Singer in the 1984 *Intermezzo* to Swallow in the 2005 *Peter Grimes;* William Dooley, Santa Fe's reigning Jochanaan in *Salome* for a decade; Doris Yarick, who was Micaela in the company's first three *Carmen* productions; John Reardon, the company's first Nick Shadow in *The Rake's Progress;* Richard Best, who sang some

THE MARRIAGE OF FIGARO
Wolfgang Amadeus Mozart
1976

Donald Gramm

THE BEGGAR'S OPERA
John Gay
1992

Elaine Bonazzi

two dozen different roles over a quarter of a century beginning in 1959; and Timothy Nolen, who has sung everything from Penderecki to Offenbach.

No singer better exemplified the Santa Fe style and standards than Donald Gramm, the brilliant American bass-baritone who sang twenty roles for the company, including Leporello, Doctor Bartolo, Nick Shadow, Papageno, Golaud, Doctor Schön in the U.S. premiere of *Lulu*, and most of all, Figaro, which he practically owned in Santa Fe—it was the first role he sang with the company in 1960 and the last as well, in 1976. For longevity and versatility, few can rival Swedish tenor Ragnar Ulfung, who has appeared with the company for twenty-six seasons starting in 1966, has taken on some two dozen roles—including the Duke in *Rigoletto,* a teacup in *L'enfant et les sortilèges,* and classic portrayals of Monostatos in *The Magic Flute* and Herod in *Salome*—and even directed the 1981 staging of *La bohème,* in which he also appeared as Benoit. Ulfung, who sang in Ingmar Bergman's famous production of *The Rake's Progress,* always suspected that it was Stravinsky who brought him to Crosby's attention; returning the favor, he regularly appeared in Santa Fe's *Rake,* first as the young hero Tom Rakewell, and then later as the auctioneer Sellem.

Although The Santa Fe Opera flourished without big names on its roster from the start, it often has caught young stars on the rise. Many of the most familiar singers of the past half century, like von Stade and Graham, got their start in Santa Fe or appeared with the company very early in their careers. One American mezzo, Suzanne Mentzer, actually decided she wanted to become an opera singer after watching the company at work night after night when she volunteered as an usher at the age of eighteen—and then sixteen years later sang Octavian in *Der Rosenkavalier* on the Santa Fe stage.

Several of the names opera lovers now know were unfamiliar at the time of their Santa Fe debuts—Catherine Malfitano as Susanna in 1973, the year before her European debut in the same role; Maria Ewing's 1975 Dorabella, just before her debuts in Salzburg and at the Met; Barbara Hendricks in *The Cunning Little Vixen* more than a decade before she sang at the Met and at La Scala; Thomas Hampson as an early-career Doctor Malatesta, before acclaimed debuts at the Vienna Staatsoper and at the Met. Alessandra Marc, an American dramatic soprano, had never sung in a professionally staged opera before she made her debut in Santa Fe as Marie in Strauss's *Friedenstag* in 1988. When Ben Heppner sang opposite Marc as Bacchus in *Ariadne auf Naxos* back

THE BARBER OF SEVILLE
Gioachino Rossini
1994

THE MAGIC FLUTE
Wolfgang Amadeus Mozart
1993

CARDILLAC
Paul Hindemith
1967

Ragnar Ulfung

THE BARBER OF SEVILLE
Gioachino Rossini
1981

Neil Rosenshein
Janice Hall

in 1990, he was just making the transition from the lyric tenor repertory to the big German roles for which he is known today. American mezzo Lorraine Hunt sang in the 1997 premiere of *Ashoka's Dream* by Peter Lieberson; she later married the composer and added his last name to hers.

George Shirley first appeared with The Santa Fe Opera singing Oedipus rex in Stravinsky's presence in 1962, shortly after making his Met debut, and continued to sing with the company nearly every year for the next decade. Swedish baritone Håkan Hagegård was best known to American audiences as Papageno in Ingmar Bergman's film of *The Magic Flute* when he came to Santa Fe for Rossini's Figaro in 1981. He returned to Santa Fe in 1998 to appear in the U.S. premiere of *A Dream Play* by his countryman Ingvar Lidholm and then in 2001 to sing the first Wozzeck of his career. Sylvia McNair sang an early-career Pamina in *The Magic Flute* in 1986 and then came back a decade later as Anne Truelove in *The Rake's Progress*, the role of her acclaimed Glyndebourne debut.

Many important young American singers have starred in key roles in Santa Fe in recent years: Elizabeth Futral as Semele, Gilda, and Zerbinetta; Mark Delavan as Germont and Simon Boccanegra; Christine Brewer, one of Gaddes's most important discoveries, as Ariadne, the Egyptian Helen, and Ellen Orford in *Peter Grimes*; Patricia Racette in an extraordinary gallery of disparate characters, from Italian heroines such as Verdi's Violetta and Amelia and Puccini's Liù to Janáček's Kátya Kabanová, Poulenc's Blanche, Tchaikovsky's Tatyana, and Picker's Emmeline—major dramatic roles in five different languages.

Although The Santa Fe Opera is identified with American singers, three international stars have made their U.S. debuts in Santa Fe. José Van Dam sang in this country for the first time in 1967 as Escamillo in Santa Fe's *Carmen*, the same role that would introduce him to the San Francisco Opera three years later and the Met in eight years. Kiri Te Kanawa was not yet a name opera lovers knew when she made her American debut in 1971 as Mozart's Countess, arguably her signature role—the role of her sensational, headline-making Covent Garden debut months later. Santa Fe heard Te Kanawa not only before New York, San Francisco, and Chicago but also before Glyndebourne, Paris, Milan, Vienna, or Salzburg. Bryn Terfel made his American debut as Figaro in Santa Fe in 1991, just as his career was about to take off. Terfel wasn't prepared for The Santa Fe Opera experience:

PETER GRIMES
Benjamin Britten
2005

Christine Brewer
James Austin Allen

LA FANCIULLA DEL WEST
Giacomo Puccini
1991

Mary Jane Johnson

•

(opposite)

THE FLYING DUTCHMAN
Richard Wagner
1988

James Morris

"I was shocked when I first arrived, because I couldn't imagine an outside opera house," the twenty-five-year-old baritone told a local reporter, "but it's such a wonderful idea, kind of an oasis."

Some of opera's biggest stars have come to Santa Fe at the height of their careers, enticed by the company's reputation and the chance to do interesting things. Revered American soprano Eleanor Steber, who had sung in the Met *Così* that first got Crosby thinking about forming an opera company, even came out of retirement from the stage to sing Miss Wingrave in the American premiere of Britten's *Owen Wingrave*. Veteran baritone Thomas Stewart broke in the role of Falstaff in Santa Fe in 1975, two summers before his wife, Evelyn Lear, sang her first Fedora with the company. Jerry Hadley had sung in major opera houses around the world before he appeared as Idomeneo in Santa Fe's first staging of Mozart's opera in 1999. Distinguished Swedish soprano Elisabeth Söderström, renowned for her portrayals of Strauss's Composer and Octavian, came to Santa Fe a quarter of a century after she made her American debut to add her definitive Christine in *Intermezzo* to the company's Strauss cycle. After singing in every other major opera house in the world, in a career nearly four decades long, Marilyn Horne added Santa Fe to the list in 1990, in one of her signature parts, Gluck's Orfeo.

American mezzo Tatiana Troyanos made her debut in Santa Fe in 1987 as Ariodante, the role with which she had inaugurated the Kennedy Center in 1971, and she returned two summers later for Cavalli's *La Calisto*. Dawn Upshaw had already won two Grammy awards and sung in the world's most prestigious houses when she decided to tackle her first Handel opera, *Xerxes*, for Santa Fe. A decade later, she returned to sing two roles written especially for her luminous soprano—the French heroine of Saariaho's *L'amour de loin*, followed by the Spanish legend Margarita Xirgu in Golijov's *Ainadamar*. French soprano Natalie Dessay was smitten with Santa Fe when she made her U.S. recital debut with The Santa Fe Opera orchestra in 2003 and she agreed at once to Gaddes's invitation to come back the very next year to sing the showstopping fireworks of Amina in Bellini's *La sonnambula*.

The backbone of The Santa Fe Opera always has been its apprentice program, and some of the singers who had the biggest impact on American opera in the second half

THE MARRIAGE OF FIGARO
Wolfgang Amadeus Mozart
1985

Brent Ellis

MITRIDATE
Wolfgang Amadeus Mozart
2001

Laura Aiken

THE GRAND DUCHESS OF GEROLSTEIN
Jacques Offenbach
1974

Richard Best · Douglas Perry

ASHOKA'S DREAM
Peter Lieberson
1997

Lorraine Hunt Lieberson

THE MARRIAGE OF FIGARO
Wolfgang Amadeus Mozart
1991

Bryn Terfel · François Loup

SEMELE
George Frideric Handel
1997

Kevin Langan

LA BELLE HÉLÈNE
Jacques Offenbach
2003

Barry Banks · Timothy Nolen

SALOME
Richard Strauss
1998

Kenneth Riegel

COSÌ FAN TUTTE
Wolfgang Amadeus Mozart
1975

Ellen Shade

of the twentieth century cut their teeth in Santa Fe. Now-celebrated bass James Morris was a Santa Fe apprentice in 1969, the year before he joined the Metropolitan Opera. He returned in 1981, already on his way to stardom, to sing Don Basilio in *The Barber of Seville* and Nick Shadow in *The Rake's Progress*. Then, in 1988, after six summers in Salzburg, Morris wanted to spend more time in his own country, and so he turned down an offer to sing Wotan in a new production of Wagner's *Ring* cycle at the Bayreuth Festival—a Wagnerian bass's touchstone role, at the Wagner shrine, no less—and came to Santa Fe instead to play the leading role in *The Flying Dutchman*, which was conducted by Edo de Waart in his American debut.

Each summer, over the course of three months, approximately forty apprentices participate in the program's whirlwind of activities: receiving voice and diction lessons; performing supporting roles; rehearsing two sets of opera scenes for public performances near the end of the season; polishing arias to sing for the opera company managers who visit each year; being coached for the starring roles they are understudying; and, in their rare off-hours, singing in local churches or even an opera-friendly piano bar. Some summers bring an unplanned star-making debut of an appren-

tice in a scenario straight out of *42nd Street*. Eudora Brown, a 2004 apprentice, was unexpectedly thrust in the spotlight when the soprano appearing as the female lead in *Beatrice and Benedict* had to withdraw a few days before opening night. Brown took over the role for the entire run, giving poised performances that delighted audiences as well as critics.

Many Santa Fe apprentices find their way back to the company once their careers take off. As a twenty-year-old apprentice in 1961, Judith Blegen sang the fleeting role of the milliner in *Der Rosenkavalier* (an opera in which she would eventually star as Sophie) and the cameo role of Barbarina in *The Marriage of Figaro*. When she returned to The Santa Fe Opera in 1969 and 1970, she had moved up to major roles, and she now sang Susanna in the Mozart opera. Samuel Ramey, who studied in Santa Fe in 1966, returned as Escamillo in *Carmen* in 1975, before he appeared in Chicago and San Francisco and at the Met, going on to become one of the most popular basses in history.

Douglas Perry returned every season for a decade after completing his apprenticeship, singing Mozart's Don Basilio and Monastatos, Puccini's Goro, Verdi's Bardolf, and a number of small roles, from a journalist in *Lulu* to the frog in *L'enfant et les sortilèges*. On the other hand, Kenneth Riegel,

ORFEO ED EURIDICE
Christoph Willibald Gluck
1990

Marilyn Horne

FEDORA
Umberto Giordano
1977

Evelyn Lear

•

(opposite)

FALSTAFF
Giuseppe Verdi
1977

Thomas Stewart

who had one small on-stage appearance in Henze's *The Stag King* when he was a company apprentice in 1965, didn't come back to Santa Fe until thirty-three years later, after he had sung with all the world's major companies, to portray Herod in *Salome*.

Some Santa Fe apprentices quickly became stars. Leona Mitchell, a 1972 apprentice, sang Mozart's Countess in Santa Fe in 1976 and went on to become a leading Verdi and Puccini soprano. Neil Shicoff, a young tenor from New York City, came to Santa Fe in the summer of 1973, sang the dramatic role of Lensky in *Eugene Onegin* with the company in 1975, and made his debut at his hometown Metropolitan Opera the next season. Chris Merritt made his Santa Fe professional debut as Doctor Caius in Verdi's *Falstaff* during the second year of his apprenticeship in 1975 and was soon opening the season at La Scala.

Over the years, the company has rewarded the singers it has helped to raise by eventually offering them opera's biggest roles. In Santa Fe, Michael Devlin played Don Giovanni and Eugene Onegin; baritone Brent Ellis sang Giorgio Germont and Figaro; soprano Ellen Shade was Mimi and Arabella; Neil Rosenshein appeared as Almaviva and Mario Cavaradossi; Ashley Putnam moved from Violetta and Lucia to the Marschallin. From time to time, the apprentice program has invited one of its graduates to return to Santa Fe to teach, bringing the process full circle. In 2005, David Holloway, who had sung several small roles with the company in the mid-seventies and enjoyed an important career in Europe and at the Met, was named director of the apprentice program that he himself entered in 1966 as an aspiring baritone from Kansas.

Today, opera stages around the world are filled with young performers who were trained in Santa Fe—Lisa Saffer, Laura Aikin, William Burden, Michelle De Young, Joyce DiDonato, Celena Shafer—and, in a time-honored fashion, many of them will continue to come back to Santa Fe. Typically, the current crop of company apprentices—forty-some each summer, their names not yet familiar to the operagoing public—have their sights set not only on the Met, Chicago, San Francisco, London, or Vienna but on returning to Santa Fe as well—on coming home.

DON PASQUALE
Gaetano Donizetti
1983

Günter von Kannen
Thomas Hampson

SIMON BOCCANEGRA
Giuseppe Verdi
2004

Mark Delavan

157

SALOME
Richard Strauss
1969

Jean Kraft

MADAME BUTTERFLY
Giacomo Puccini
1965

Benjamin Rayson
Mildred Allen
Douglas Scott

THE BARBER OF SEVILLE

Gioachino Rossini

1967

Helen Vanni

John Reardon

CARMEN

Georges Bizet

1967

Regina Sarfaty

LA CALISTO
Pier Francesco Cavalli
1989

Joanne Kolomyjec

FROM CLASSICS
TO RARITIES

DON GIOVANNI
*Wolfgang Amadeus
Mozart*
2004

Ying Huang
Mariusz Kwiecien

The Santa Fe Opera has performed more operas by Richard Strauss than by Puccini, more by Henze than Verdi. It has staged *Simon Boccanegra,* but not *Aida* or *Il trovatore.* It has presented *Turandot* only once, but Stravinsky's *Le rossignol* five times. It has done *The Rake's Progress* more often than *Tosca.* It has produced Ambroise Thomas's *Mignon,* but not Gounod's *Faust.* It has presented just one Wagner opera, but four by Handel and three by Pier Francesco Cavalli. Of the twenty most frequently performed operas in the United States, according to Opera America's "top twenty" statistics, four have never been produced in Santa Fe at all.

In half a century, The Santa Fe Opera has never fit the standard opera house profile. The range of what it can do comfortably spans the styles of three centuries, covering everything from pre-Mozart opera to the newly commissioned; from the seriousness of *Wozzeck* to the delectable froth of Offenbach's *La belle Hélène;* from interior dramas such as Saariaho's *L'amour de loin,* with only three characters on stage for the entire evening, to the wide-angle panorama of *Turandot* and the grand-opera spectacle of *Simon Boccanegra.* From the start, the company has ignored operas that are overplayed, in effect challenging the complacency of mainstream programming—what opera critic Joseph Kerman

has called the hardening of the repertory. In 1984, when ticket sales were off and one local hotel manager publicly wondered if the summer's fare of unusually obscure works wasn't responsible for a drop in tourism, Crosby responded by announcing an equally adventurous season for 1985—and ticket sales rebounded.

Italian opera, the staple of many American companies, has never been a Santa Fe priority. When the company was founded, Verdi was the most frequently performed opera composer in America, but over the years Santa Fe has staged just five of Verdi's operas, and of those, only *La traviata* has been performed with any regularity. Puccini has been more fully represented, and *Madame Butterfly* holds a special place in the company's history, having been picked to inaugurate not only the first theater but both of the new houses later built on the same spot.

Like Glyndebourne and Salzburg, The Santa Fe Opera has always placed Mozart's operas at the heart of its repertory, beginning with the first season's *Così fan tutte.* An opera by Mozart was on the schedule every year in Santa Fe until the late seventies—nearly all of them conducted by Robert Baustian, who was a pillar of the musical staff for some two decades and helped to set the company's high standards from the start. (Baustian led *The Tower* and *The Barber of Seville*

COSÌ FAN TUTTE
Wolfgang Amadeus Mozart
2003

Troy Cook
Patricia Risley
Ana María Martínez
Charles Castronovo

LA BELLE HÉLÈNE
Jacques Offenbach
2003

Susan Graham
William Burden

THE ITALIAN GIRL IN
ALGIERS
Gioachino Rossini
2002

Stephanie Blythe
Apprentice Ensemble

Karen Beck
Ashley Putnam
Aviva Orvath

Marla McDaniels
Linn Maxwell
Joseph McKee

Billie Nash
Gene Ives
Linn Maxwell
Jimmie Lu Null

MADAME BUTTERFLY
Giacomo Puccini
1998

Judith Christin
James Austin Allen

Costume designs by Robert Indiana.

THE MOTHER OF US ALL
Virgil Thomson
1976

Thomas Parker   Jimmie Lu Null
Batyah Godfrey   Mignon Dunn
James Atherton   Linn Maxwell

WOZZECK
Alban Berg
2001

Anne Schwanewilms
Håkan Hagegård

the first season and later presided over the American premieres of two Henze operas and *The Cunning Little Vixen.*) The company has staged *The Marriage of Figaro* more often than any other work, but in recent years under Gaddes's guidance, it also has turned out stylish, dazzlingly sung productions of lesser-known Mozart, from *Mitridate* and *Lucio Silla,* the works of a precocious teenager, to *La clemenza di Tito,* the composer's final opera, premiered just three months before he died.

The Santa Fe Opera contributed to the wave of interest in baroque opera early on, with the first staged performances of Pier Francesco Cavalli's *L'Egisto* in more than three hundred years. The resurgence of interest in Cavalli was launched almost single-handedly by the Glyndebourne Festival's 1967 production of *Ormindo,* in a compelling edition by English conductor Raymond Leppard, and Santa Fe asked him to prepare *L'Egisto,* which was last known to have been produced in Venice in 1643. Working with a nearly illegible seventeenth-century manuscript, Leppard reconstructed and orchestrated *L'Egisto* and then came to Santa Fe to make his American debut conducting the opera. *L'Egisto* was the surprise hit of the 1974 season, and Leppard was back in 1983 to work similar wonders on Cavalli's *L'Orione,* another American premiere. With Santa Fe in the forefront of

an international Cavalli revival, in 1989 the company staged *La Calisto,* starring Tatiana Troyanos as the goddess Diana. In 1986, Santa Fe had moved even farther back in time when it produced *The Coronation of Poppea* by Cavalli's teacher, Claudio Monteverdi. The oldest opera in the company's repertory, *Poppea* was the last work Bliss Hebert staged in Santa Fe, capping a thirty-year association that began with *The Rake's Progress* for the opening season and included the company's first *Pelléas et Mélisande,* the premiere of Henze's *The Stag King,* and works by Mozart, Ravel, Schoenberg, and Offenbach.

From Monteverdi and Cavalli, it was a logical leap forward to Handel, whose operas were beginning to receive serious attention, when Santa Fe staged *Ariodante* in 1987, performed nearly uncut, which was unusual at the time. There were particularly strong performances from Troyanos, back to sing the lead, a commanding trouser role, and from Benita Valente as Ariodante's fiancée. The Handel opera marked the company debut of director John Copley, who worked in Santa Fe almost every season for the next decade. Six years later, the company staged *Xerxes,* conducted by Kenneth Montgomery and featuring Dawn Upshaw and Frederica von Stade, who were both appearing in a Handel opera for the first time. By the time The Santa Fe Opera offered *Semele* in 1997 and

WOZZECK
Alban Berg
2001

Håkan Hagegård
Anthony Laciura

PETER GRIMES
Benjamin Britten
2005

Apprentice Ensemble

THE MAGIC FLUTE
Wolfgang Amadeus Mozart
1998

Heidi Grant Murphy
Ingela Onstad
Jennifer Dawn Hines
Julie Bartholomew

LA SONNAMBULA
Vincenzo Bellini
2004

Natalie Dessay
Shalva Mukeria
Apprentice Ensemble

LA CLEMENZA DI TITO
Wolfgang Amadeus Mozart
2002

Joyce DiDonato
Isabel Bayrakdarian

Agrippina in 2004, Handel operas were no longer just curiosities; they were now even audience favorites.

The Santa Fe Opera has never relied on the nineteenth-century classics for the backbone of its repertory, but it has offered its audiences rare glimpses of lesser-known works of the period, beginning with Donizetti's *Anna Bolena* in the company's 1959 season—billed at the time as the first U.S. staging of the opera in nearly one hundred years. Although it has presented *The Barber of Seville* at least once in each of its five decades, it also has staged Rossini's less familiar *Count Ory* in 1978, followed by *Ermione* in 2000. In the eighties, The Santa Fe Opera mounted two French Romantic rarities, Ambroise Thomas's *Mignon* and Jules Massenet's *Chérubin,* and more recently it struck gold with a witty and stylish staging of Berlioz's *Beatrice and Benedict.*

By 1976, the year of the American bicentennial, regional opera companies in America had performed Virgil Thomson's *The Mother of Us All* nearly a thousand times. But the big houses had steered away from this quintessentially American opera, with its episodic tale of feminism ("It has no plot," Thomson said, matter-of-factly), its playful Gertrude Stein libretto, and its large cast with just one major role. The

ORPHEUS IN
THE UNDERWORLD
Jacques Offenbach
1985

Kathryn Gamberoni

opera hadn't been staged in New York since its premiere there in 1947. In other words, it was a natural for Santa Fe. The company did itself proud, particularly in its pairing of Thomson's quirky, homespun music with iconic set and costume designs by visual artist Robert Indiana. The production was underwritten by Robert L. B. Tobin, who had a lifelong interest in stage design.

Indiana and Peter Wood, the Tony Award–winning director of Tom Stoppard's *Travesties,* turned Thomson's opera into a grand Fourth of July pageant, complete with fireworks, brightly colored floats, and a Model T that drove across the stage. The characters wore Miss America–style sashes printed with their names. Mignon Dunn, better known for singing big roles at houses like the Met, was an imposing Susan B. Anthony, the centerpiece of a strong ensemble show. Before *The Mother of Us All* closed, the Santa Fe cast and orchestra, under the baton of Raymond Leppard, gathered in the local Armory for the Arts to make a studio recording, the first ever of this quintessential American opera.

Over the years, The Santa Fe Opera has done well by the classics of modern opera. The company produced both Berg's *Wozzeck,* staged by Lotfi Mansouri, and Poulenc's *Dialogues of the Carmelites,* directed by Vera Zorina, for the first time

DIALOGUES OF THE CARMELITES
Francis Poulenc
1999

Christine Goerke

COSÍ FAN TUTTE
Wolfgang Amadeus Mozart
1988

Judith Christen
Claude Corbeil

BEATRICE AND BENEDICT
Hector Berlioz
2004

William Burden
Eudora Brown

Kristine Jepson
Christine Goerke

Corey McKern
Christine Goerke

AGRIPPINA
George Frideric Handel
2004

David Walker
Christine Goerke

Lisa Saffer
Christine Goerke

AGRIPPINA
George Frideric Handel
2004

Christine Goerke
Christophe Dumaux

during its tenth season—remarkably, the same year it revived *The Rake's Progress* and *Capriccio*. Six years later, it presented its first *Pelléas et Mélisande,* Debussy's only opera. More recently, it offered *Kátya Kabanová* and *Peter Grimes*—both triumphs, musically and dramatically, that showed the company doing what it does best.

In 2005, the company presented an extensively revised version of Osvaldo Golijov's *Ainadamar,* which had premiered at Tanglewood two summers before. With the entire creative team in town during the weeks before the opening—including Golijov, the Argentine-born American composer; his librettist, David Henry Hwang; director Peter Sellars; and their muse, Dawn Upshaw, the singer for whom the score was written— *Ainadamar* literally became a living work of art, being rewritten and rehearsed day by day. Golijov is one of the composers who will navigate the course of serious music in the twenty-first century, and *Ainadamar* is unmistakably a new kind of opera for a still-young century. It has little in the way of a conventional plot and the score is an unlikely mix of everything from salsa and flamenco to Straussian lyricism, recalling Golijov's immersion in *Daphne* as he was writing. Santa Fe's production was spare and unconventional—the set a single, vast *Guernica*-like canvas that Gronk, a Los

THE MARRIAGE OF FIGARO
Wolfgang Amadeus Mozart
1985

Mary Jane Johnson
Faith Esham
Susan Quittmeyer

Angeles–based artist, painted on-site, using hardware-store brushes and four gallons of paint. The costumes, seemingly off the rack, were plain black dresses, a brilliant blue suit, and camouflage fatigues that had been purchased in an Albuquerque army supply store.

In its early days, The Santa Fe Opera couldn't risk scheduling more than two performances of a new work, but the company sold out all six nights of *Ainadamar.* In 2005, this was the opera everyone wanted to see and talk about. *Ainadamar* is a good barometer of how far The Santa Fe Opera has come in five decades, as well as a yardstick of how different the musical world is today. It also is a reminder that the company still loves to take bold steps—to shake things up. By staging *Ainadamar,* Santa Fe was asking the questions that any enterprising opera company should be raising early in the twenty-first century: Where is opera heading, and what comes next? Today The Santa Fe Opera is still driven by curiosity, adventure, and the promise of something new—by the idea of "possibility" that set the company in motion half a century ago. Under the sliver of a Santa Fe moon—the *fermata,* as García Lorca called it, the musical symbol for pausing—opera is poised to move on.

KÁTYA KABANOVÁ
Leoš Janáček
2002

Patricia Racette

LUCIO SILLA
Wolfgang Amadeus Mozart
2005

Celena Shafer
Gregory Kunde
Susan Graham

AINADAMAR
Osvaldo Golijov
2005

Dawn Upshaw
Jessica Rivera
Kelley O'Connor
Apprentice Ensemble

AINADAMAR
Osvaldo Golijov
2005

Dawn Upshaw

REPERTORY, 1957–2006

1957   *Madame Butterfly*, Giacomo Puccini
Così fan tutte, Wolfgang Amadeus Mozart
La serva padrona, Giovanni Battista Pergolesi
The Tower, Marvin David Levy
The Barber of Seville, Gioachino Rossini
Ariadne auf Naxos, Richard Strauss
The Rake's Progress, Igor Stravinsky

1958   *La bohème*, Giacomo Puccini
Così fan tutte, Wolfgang Amadeus Mozart
Falstaff, Giuseppe Verdi
Wuthering Heights, Carlisle Floyd
Cinderella, Gioachino Rossini
Capriccio, Richard Strauss

1959   *Die Fledermaus*, Johann Strauss
Anna Bolena, Gaetano Donizetti
Madame Butterfly, Giacomo Puccini
The Abduction from the Seraglio, Wolfgang Amadeus Mozart
The Barber of Seville, Gioachino Rossini
Regina, Marc Blitzstein

1960   *The Gondoliers*, Arthur Sullivan
La traviata, Giuseppe Verdi
Cinderella, Gioachino Rossini
Oedipus rex, Igor Stravinsky
Gianni Schicchi, Giacomo Puccini
The Rake's Progress, Igor Stravinsky
Tosca, Giacomo Puccini
The Marriage of Figaro, Wolfgang Amadeus Mozart

1961   *Carmen*, Georges Bizet
Der Rosenkavalier, Richard Strauss
La bohème, Giacomo Puccini
Oedipus rex, Igor Stravinsky
Perséphone, Igor Stravinsky
The Ballad of Baby Doe, Douglas Moore
The Marriage of Figaro, Wolfgang Amadeus Mozart
News of the Day, Paul Hindemith

1962   *Salome*, Richard Strauss
Così fan tutte, Wolfgang Amadeus Mozart
La traviata, Giuseppe Verdi
Joan of Arc at the Stake, Arthur Honegger

     Mavra, Le rossignol, Renard, Igor Stravinsky
Oedipus rex, Igor Stravinsky
Perséphone, Igor Stravinsky
The Rake's Progress, Igor Stravinsky
Tosca, Giacomo Puccini

1963   *Lulu*, Alban Berg
Joan of Arc at the Stake, Arthur Honegger
Don Giovanni, Wolfgang Amadeus Mozart
Madame Butterfly, Giacomo Puccini
L'enfant et les sortilèges, Maurice Ravel
Le rossignol, Igor Stravinsky
Die Fledermaus, Johann Strauss
Der Rosenkavalier, Richard Strauss

1964   *Rigoletto*, Giuseppe Verdi
The Marriage of Figaro, Wolfgang Amadeus Mozart
Carmen, Georges Bizet
Gianni Schicchi, Giacomo Puccini
L'enfant et les sortilèges, Maurice Ravel
Daphne, Richard Strauss
La bohème, Giacomo Puccini
Lulu, Alban Berg

1965   *La traviata*, Giuseppe Verdi
The Barber of Seville, Gioachino Rossini
Madame Butterfly, Giacomo Puccini
Lucia di Lammermoor, Gaetano Donizetti
Arabella, Richard Strauss
The Stag King, Hans Werner Henze
The Nose, Dmitri Shostakovich
The Marriage of Figaro, Wolfgang Amadeus Mozart

1966   *Tosca*, Giacomo Puccini
Cinderella, Gioachino Rossini
Don Giovanni, Wolfgang Amadeus Mozart
Dialogues of the Carmelites, Francis Poulenc
The Rake's Progress, Igor Stravinsky
Capriccio, Richard Strauss
Rigoletto, Giuseppe Verdi
Wozzeck, Alban Berg

1967   *Carmen*, Georges Bizet
La bohème, Giacomo Puccini

The Barber of Seville, Gioachino Rossini
Cardillac, Paul Hindemith
Boulevard Solitude, Hans Werner Henze
The Marriage of Figaro, Wolfgang Amadeus Mozart
Salome, Richard Strauss

1968 *Madame Butterfly*, Giacomo Puccini
The Magic Flute, Wolfgang Amadeus Mozart
La traviata, Giuseppe Verdi
The Elixir of Love, Gaetano Donizetti
Der Rosenkavalier, Richard Strauss
The Bassarids, Hans Werner Henze
Perséphone, Igor Stravinsky
Die Jakobsleiter, Arnold Schoenberg

1969 *Tosca*, Giacomo Puccini
Così fan tutte, Wolfgang Amadeus Mozart
The Magic Flute, Wolfgang Amadeus Mozart
Le rossignol, Igor Stravinsky
Help, Help, The Globolinks!, Gian Carlo Menotti
Salome, Richard Strauss
The Devils of Loudon, Krzysztof Penderecki

1970 *La traviata*, Giuseppe Verdi
Le rossignol, Igor Stravinsky
Help, Help, The Globolinks!, Gian Carlo Menotti
The Marriage of Figaro, Wolfgang Amadeus Mozart
Anna Bolena, Gaetano Donizetti
The Rake's Progress, Igor Stravinsky
Opera, Luciano Berio

1971 *Don Carlos*, Giuseppe Verdi
The Magic Flute, Wolfgang Amadeus Mozart
The Grand Duchess of Gerolstein, Jacques Offenbach
The Marriage of Figaro, Wolfgang Amadeus Mozart
The Flying Dutchman, Richard Wagner
Yerma, Heitor Villa-Lobos

1972 *The Grand Duchess of Gerolstein*, Jacques Offenbach
Madame Butterfly, Giacomo Puccini
Don Giovanni, Wolfgang Amadeus Mozart
Pelléas et Mélisande, Claude Debussy
Salome, Richard Strauss
Melusine, Aribert Reimann

1973 *La bohème*, Giacomo Puccini
The Marriage of Figaro, Wolfgang Amadeus Mozart
The Merry Widow, Franz Lehár
The Flying Dutchman, Richard Wagner
Le rossignol, Igor Stravinsky
L'enfant et les sortilèges, Maurice Ravel
Owen Wingrave, Benjamin Britten

1974 *La bohème*, Giacomo Puccini
The Magic Flute, Wolfgang Amadeus Mozart
The Grand Duchess of Gerolstein, Jacques Offenbach
Lulu, Alban Berg
L'Egisto, Pier Francesco Cavalli

1975 *Carmen*, Georges Bizet
Falstaff, Giuseppe Verdi
Così fan tutte, Wolfgang Amadeus Mozart
La vida breve, Manuel de Falla
L'enfant et les sortilèges, Maurice Ravel
The Cunning Little Vixen, Leoš Janáček

1976 *La traviata*, Giuseppe Verdi
The Marriage of Figaro, Wolfgang Amadeus Mozart
L'Egisto, Pier Francesco Cavalli
Salome, Richard Strauss
The Mother of Us All, Virgil Thomson

1977 *The Italian Straw Hat*, Nino Rota
Falstaff, Giuseppe Verdi
Pelléas et Mélisande, Claude Debussy
Fedora, Umberto Giordano
Così fan tutte, Wolfgang Amadeus Mozart

1978 *Tosca*, Giacomo Puccini
Count Ory, Gioachino Rossini
Eugene Onegin, Peter Ilyich Tchaikovsky
Salome, Richard Strauss
The Duchess of Malfi, Stephen Oliver

1979 *The Grand Duchess of Gerolstein*, Jacques Offenbach
Lucia di Lammermoor, Gaetano Donizetti
The Magic Flute, Wolfgang Amadeus Mozart
Lulu, Alban Berg
Salome, Richard Strauss

1980   *La traviata*, Giuseppe Verdi
        The Magic Flute, Wolfgang Amadeus Mozart
        Eugene Onegin, Peter Ilyich Tchaikovsky
        Erwartung, Von Heute auf Morgen, Die Jakobsleiter,
           Arnold Schoenberg
        Elektra, Richard Strauss

1981   *La bohème*, Giacomo Puccini
        The Barber of Seville, Gioachino Rossini
        Daphne, Richard Strauss
        The Rake's Progress, Igor Stravinsky
        News of the Day, Paul Hindemith

1982   *Die Fledermaus*, Johann Strauss
        The Marriage of Figaro, Wolfgang Amadeus Mozart
        Mignon, Ambroise Thomas
        Die Liebe der Danae, Richard Strauss
        The Confidence Man, George Rochberg

1983   *Orpheus in the Underworld*, Jacques Offenbach
        Don Pasquale, Gaetano Donizetti
        Arabella, Richard Strauss
        L'Orione, Pier Francesco Cavalli
        The Turn of the Screw, Benjamin Britten

1984   *A Florentine Tragedy*, Alexander von Zemlinsky
        Violanta, Erich Wolfgang Korngold
        The Magic Flute, Wolfgang Amadeus Mozart
        Il matrimonio segreto, Domenico Cimarosa
        Intermezzo, Richard Strauss
        We Come to the River, Hans Werner Henze

1985   *Orpheus in the Underworld*, Jacques Offenbach
        The Marriage of Figaro, Wolfgang Amadeus Mozart
        The English Cat, Hans Werner Henze
        Die Liebe der Danae, Richard Strauss
        The Tempest, John Eaton

1986   *Die Fledermaus*, Johann Strauss
        The Magic Flute, Wolfgang Amadeus Mozart
        The Coronation of Poppea, Claudio Monteverdi
        The Egyptian Helen, Richard Strauss
        The King Goes Forth to France, Aulis Sallinen

1987   *Madame Butterfly*, Giacomo Puccini
        The Marriage of Figaro, Wolfgang Amadeus Mozart
        Ariodante, George Frideric Handel
        Die schweigsame Frau, Richard Strauss
        The Nose, Dmitri Shostakovich

1988   *Die Fledermaus*, Johann Strauss
        Così fan tutte, Wolfgang Amadeus Mozart
        The Flying Dutchman, Richard Wagner
        Feuersnot, Friedenstag, Richard Strauss
        The Black Mask, Krzysztof Penderecki

1989   *La traviata*, Giuseppe Verdi
        La Calisto, Pier Francesco Cavalli
        Chérubin, Jules Massenet
        Der Rosenkavalier, Richard Strauss
        A Night at the Chinese Opera, Judith Weir

1990   *La bohème*, Giacomo Puccini
        Così fan tutte, Wolfgang Amadeus Mozart
        Orfeo ed Euridice, Christoph Willibald Gluck
        Ariadne auf Naxos, Richard Strauss
        Judith, Siegfried Matthus

1991   *La traviata*, Giuseppe Verdi
        The Marriage of Figaro, Wolfgang Amadeus Mozart
        La fanciulla del West, Giacomo Puccini
        Die schweigsame Frau, Richard Strauss
        Oedipus, Wolfgang Rihm

1992   *Die Fledermaus*, Johann Strauss
        Don Giovanni, Wolfgang Amadeus Mozart
        The Beggar's Opera, John Gay
        Der Rosenkavalier, Richard Strauss
        The Sorrows of Young Werther, Hans-Jürgen von Bose

1993   *La bohème*, Giacomo Puccini
        The Magic Flute, Wolfgang Amadeus Mozart
        Xerxes, George Frideric Handel
        Capriccio, Richard Strauss
        The Protagonist, The Tsar Has His Photograph Taken,
           Kurt Weill

1994   *Tosca*, Giacomo Puccini
        The Barber of Seville, Gioachino Rossini
        The Abduction from the Seraglio, Wolfgang Amadeus Mozart
        Intermezzo, Richard Strauss
        Blond Eckbert, Judith Weir

1995   *Countess Maritza*, Emmerich Kálmán
        The Marriage of Figaro, Wolfgang Amadeus Mozart
        La fanciulla del West, Giacomo Puccini
        Salome, Richard Strauss
        Modern Painters, David Lang

1996   *Madame Butterfly*, Giacomo Puccini
        Don Giovanni, Wolfgang Amadeus Mozart
        The Rake's Progress, Igor Stravinsky
        Daphne, Richard Strauss
        Emmeline, Tobias Picker
        Noah's Flood, Benjamin Britten (Santa Maria
            de la Paz Catholic church)

1997   *La traviata*, Giuseppe Verdi
        Così fan tutte, Wolfgang Amadeus Mozart
        Semele, George Frideric Handel
        Arabella, Richard Strauss
        Ashoka's Dream, Peter Lieberson

1998   *Madame Butterfly*, Giacomo Puccini
        The Magic Flute, Wolfgang Amadeus Mozart
        Beatrice and Benedict, Hector Berlioz
        Salome, Richard Strauss
        A Dream Play, Ingvar Lidholm

1999   *Countess Maritza*, Emmerich Kálmán
        Carmen, Georges Bizet
        Idomeneo, Wolfgang Amadeus Mozart
        Ariadne auf Naxos, Richard Strauss
        Dialogues of the Carmelites, Francis Poulenc
        Noah's Flood, Benjamin Britten (Our Lady of the
            Most Holy Rosary Catholic church)

2000   *Rigoletto*, Giuseppe Verdi
        The Marriage of Figaro, Wolfgang Amadeus Mozart
        Ermione, Gioachino Rossini

        Elektra, Richard Strauss
        Venus and Adonis, Hans Werner Henze
        The Beggar's Opera, John Gay (El Museo Cultural)

2001   *Lucia di Lammermoor*, Gaetano Donizetti
        Falstaff, Giuseppe Verdi
        Mitridate, Wolfgang Amadeus Mozart
        The Egyptian Helen, Richard Strauss
        Wozzeck, Alban Berg
        H.M.S. Pinafore, Arthur Sullivan (Lensic Theater)

2002   *Eugene Onegin*, Peter Ilyich Tchaikovsky
        The Italian Girl in Algiers, Gioachino Rossini
        La clemenza di Tito, Wolfgang Amadeus Mozart
        La traviata, Giuseppe Verdi
        L'amour de loin, Kaija Saariaho
        The Pirates of Penzance, Arthur Sullivan (Lensic Theater)

2003   *La belle Hélène*, Jacques Offenbach
        Così fan tutte, Wolfgang Amadeus Mozart
        Intermezzo, Richard Strauss
        Kátya Kabanová, Leoš Janáček
        Madame Mao, Bright Sheng

2004   *Simon Boccanegra*, Giuseppe Verdi
        Don Giovanni, Wolfgang Amadeus Mozart
        Beatrice and Benedict, Hector Berlioz
        Agrippina, George Frideric Handel
        La sonnambula, Vincenzo Bellini

2005   *Turandot*, Giacomo Puccini
        The Barber of Seville, Gioachino Rossini
        Lucio Silla, Wolfgang Amadeus Mozart
        Peter Grimes, Benjamin Britten
        Ainadamar, Osvaldo Golijov

2006   *Carmen*, Georges Bizet
        The Magic Flute, Wolfgang Amadeus Mozart
        Cinderella, Jules Massenet
        Salome, Richard Strauss
        The Tempest, Thomas Adès

Commissioned Works

1958	*Wuthering Heights,* Carlisle Floyd
1970	*Opera,* Luciano Berio
1982	*The Confidence Man,* George Rochberg
1985	*The Tempest,* John Eaton
1995	*Modern Painters,* David Lang
1996	*Emmeline,* Tobias Picker
1997	*Ashoka's Dream,* Peter Lieberson
2003	*Madame Mao,* Bright Sheng

World Premieres

1957	*The Tower,* Marvin David Levy
1971	*Yerma,* Heitor Villa-Lobos

American Premieres

1958	*Capriccio,* Richard Strauss
1961	*News of the Day,* Paul Hindemith
1961	*Perséphone,* Igor Stravinsky
1963	*Lulu,* Acts 1 and 2, Alban Berg
1964	*Daphne,* Richard Strauss
1965	*The Stag King,* Hans Werner Henze
1965	*The Nose,* Dmitri Shostakovich
1967	*Boulevard Solitude,* Hans Werner Henze
1967	*Cardillac,* Paul Hindemith
1968	*The Bassarids,* Hans Werner Henze
1968	*Die Jakobsleiter,* Arnold Schoenberg
1969	*Help, Help, The Globolinks!,* Gian Carlo Menotti
1969	*The Devils of Loudon,* Krzysztof Penderecki
1972	*Melusine,* Aribert Reimann
1973	*Owen Wingrave,* Benjamin Britten
1974	*L'Egisto,* Pier Francesco Cavalli
1975	*The Cunning Little Vixen,* Leoš Janáček
1977	*The Italian Straw Hat,* Nino Rota
1978	*The Duchess of Malfi,* Stephen Oliver
1979	*Lulu,* with Act 3, Alban Berg
1980	*Von Heute auf Morgen,* Arnold Schoenberg
1982	*Die Liebe der Danae,* Richard Strauss
1983	*L'Orione,* Pier Francesco Cavalli
1984	*We Come to the River,* Hans Werner Henze
1984	*Intermezzo,* Richard Strauss
1984	*A Florentine Tragedy,* Alexander von Zemlinsky
1985	*The English Cat,* Hans Werner Henze
1986	*The King Goes Forth to France,* Aulis Sallinen
1986	*The Egyptian Helen,* Richard Strauss
1988	*The Black Mask,* Krzysztof Penderecki
1988	*Friedenstag,* Richard Strauss
1989	*A Night at the Chinese Opera,* Judith Weir
1990	*Judith,* Siegfried Matthus
1991	*Oedipus,* Wolfgang Rihm
1992	*The Sorrows of Young Werther,* Hans-Jürgen von Bose
1993	*The Protagonist,* Kurt Weill
1993	*The Tsar Has His Photograph Taken,* Kurt Weill
1994	*Blond Eckbert,* Judith Weir
1998	*A Dream Play,* Ingvar Lidholm
2000	*Venus and Adonis,* Hans Werner Henze
2002	*L'amour de loin,* Kaija Saariaho
2006	*The Tempest,* Thomas Adès

PHOTOGRAPHY CREDITS

L = left; C = center; R = right; A = above;
B = below; AL = above left, AR = above right;
BL = below left; BR = below right

Page 1	Eliot Porter	Page 55A	Ken Howard	Page 98	David Stein
Page 2	Eliot Porter	Page 55B	David Stein	Page 99	David Stein
Page 3	Eliot Porter	Page 57	Ken Howard	Page 100	Hans Fahrmeyer
Pages 4/5	Ken Howard	Page 58	Tony Perry	Page 101	Hans Fahrmeyer
Page 6	Mark Nohl	Page 59	Tony Perry	Page 102	Hans Fahrmeyer
Page 8	Yusef Karsh	Page 60	Tony Perry	Page 103	Hans Fahrmeyer
Page 11	Hans Farhmeyer	Page 61	Tony Perry	Page 104	Hans Fahrmeyer
Page 15	David Stein	Page 62	Tony Perry	Page 105	Ken Howard
Page 16	Scott Humbert	Page 63	Unknown	Page 106	Hans Fahrmeyer
Page 17	Unknown	Page 64	Tony Perry	Page 107	Michael Rosenthal
Page 18	Scott Humbert	Page 65	Tony Perry	Page 108	Hans Fahrmeyer
Page 19	Scott Humbert	Page 66	Cradoc Bagshaw	Page 109	Hans Fahrmeyer
Page 20	Robert Godwin	Page 67	Martin Weil	Page 111	Paul Slaughter
Page 21	Robert Godwin	Page 68	Tony Perry	Page 112	LeGaunt
Page 22	Robert Godwin	Page 69	David Stein	Page 113	LeGaunt
Page 23	Paul Horpedahl	Page 71	Robert Reck	Page 114	David Stein
Page 24	Robert Godwin	Page 72	Unknown	Page 115	David Stein
Page 25	Sophy Rickett	Page 73	Alan Stoker	Page 116	David Stein
Page 26	Paul Horpedahl	Page 74	David Stein	Page 117	David Stein
Page 27	Paul Horpedahl	Page 75	Unknown	Page 118	Ken Howard
Page 30	Unknown	Page 76	Hans Fahrmeyer	Page 119	Michael Rosenthal
Page 32	T. Harmon Parkhurst	Page 77	Hans Fahrmeyer	Page 120	Hans Fahrmeyer
Page 34	Edward Weston	Page 78	Dan Barsotti	Page 121	Ken Howard
Page 39	Unknown	Page 79	Robert Reck	Page 122	Hans Fahrmeyer
Page 40	Unknown	Page 80	Robert Godwin	Page 123	Ken Howard
Page 41	Unknown	Page 81	Ken Howard	Page 124	Michael Mouchette
Page 42	Unknown	Page 82L	Dan Barsotti	Page 125	Michael Mouchette
Page 43	Unknown	Page 82C	Michael Rosenthal	Page 126	Michael Mouchette
Page 44	Dean Brown	Page 82R	Dan Barsotti	Page 127	Michael Mouchette
Page 45	Tyler Dingee	Page 83	Dan Barsotti	Page 128	David Stein
Page 46	Unknown	Page 84	Michael Rosenthal	Page 129	David Stein
Page 47	Laura Gilpin	Page 85	Dan Barsotti	Page 130	Hans Fahrmeyer
Page 48	Tony Perry	Page 86	Dan Barsotti	Page 131	Paul Slaughter
Page 49	Unknown	Page 87	Michael Mouchette	Page 132	Paul Slaughter
Page 50	Hans Fahrmeyer	Page 88	Ken Howard	Page 133	Ken Howard
Page 51	Ken Howard	Page 89	Ken Howard	Page 134	Ken Howard
Page 52	Unknown	Page 90	Robert Godwin	Page 135	Ken Howard
Page 53	Ken Howard	Page 91	Dan Barsotti	Page 137	Ken Howard
Page 54	Scott Humbert	Page 92	Robert Reck	Page 138	Hans Fahrmeyer
		Pages 92/3	Robert Godwin	Page 139	Ken Howard
		Page 94	Hans Fahrmeyer	Page 140	Robert Baxter
		Page 95	Dan Barsotti	Page 141	Robert Nugent
		Page 97	Ken Howard	Page 142	Alan Stoker

ACKNOWLEDGMENTS

MUSEUMS

The use of the following photographs and paintings are courtesy of:

AMON CARTER MUSEUM
Page 1: Eliot Porter (1901–1990); *Cloud Formations, Tesuque, New Mexico, May 1978*; © Amon Carter Museum.

Page 2: Eliot Porter; *Sunset Clouds, Tesuque, New Mexico, 1960*; © Amon Carter Museum.

Page 3: Eliot Porter; *Moon and Evening Clouds, Tesuque, New Mexico, 1977*; © Amon Carter Museum.

Page 47: Laura Gilpin (1891–1979); *The Santa Fe Opera Theater, 1957*; © Amon Carter Museum.

THE ART INSTITUTE OF CHICAGO, THE ALFRED STEIGLITZ COLLECTION
Page 29: Marsden Hartley (1877–1943); *Landscape #3, Cash Entry Mines, New Mexico*.

MABEL DODGE LUHAN COLLECTION, YALE COLLECTION OF AMERICAN LITERATURE, BEINECKE RARE BOOKS AND MANUSCRIPT LIBRARY

Page 30: Unknown; *Mabel Dodge Luhan and Tony Luhan, Taos, New Mexico, 1948*; © Yale Committee on Literary Property, c/o Curator of American Literature, Beinecke Rare Books and Manuscript Library.

FRED JONES JR. MUSEUM OF ART, UNIVERSITY OF OKLAHOMA
Page 31: B. J. O. Nordfeldt (1878–1955); *Thunder Dancing, 1928*.

FRAY ANGÉLICO CHÁVEZ HISTORICAL ARCHIVES, PALACE OF THE GOVERNORS, MUSEUM OF NEW MEXICO
Page 32: T. Harmon Parkhurst (1883–1952); *John Sloan standing in front of his easel on right, his wife sitting in a car on left, with Sun and Moon mountains in the background, 1926*; © Chávez Historical Archives.

ANSCHUTZ COLLECTION
Page 28: Marsden Hartley (1877–1943); *Landscape No. 3 (Cash Entry Mines, New Mexico), 1920*.

Page 33: John Sloan (1871–1951); *Chama Running Red, 1925*.

MUSEUM OF FINE ARTS, MUSEUM OF NEW MEXICO, DEPARTMENT OF CULTURAL AFFAIRS
Page 6: Mark Knol (b. 1950); Moonset, Valle Grande, New Mexico.

Page 34: Edward Weston (1886–1958); *The Santa Fe to Albuquerque Road, 1937*; © 1981 Edward Weston Archives, Center for Creative Photography, Arizona Board of Regents.

Page 35: Leon Kroll (1884–1974); *Santa Fe Hills, 1917*.

Page 36: Georgia O'Keeffe (1887–1986); *Red Hills with the Pedernales, 1936*; © Artists Rights Society (ARS), New York.

Page 37: John Sloan (1871–1951); *Music in the Plaza, 1920*; © Museum of Fine Arts, Santa Fe.

Page 166: Robert Indiana (b. 1928); Six cut paper costume and scenery designs for *The Mother of Us All*; © 2001 Morgan Art Foundation Ltd./Artists Rights Society (ARS), New York.

SPECIAL THANKS

The Santa Fe Opera wishes to express its gratitude to the following individuals
for their help and encouragement in the preparation of this book:

Nico Castel

Thomas and June Catron

Matthew Epstein

Susan Graham

Thomas Jaehn, Curator, Fray Chavez History Library, Santa Fe

Donald Lamm

Richard Lampert, Zaplin-Lampert Gallery, Santa Fe

Miranda Masocco Levy

Susan Morris

Regina Sarfaty Rickless

Joan Tafoya, Registrar, Museum of Fine Arts, Santa Fe

Helen Vanni

Steven Yates, Curator of Photography, Museum of Fine Arts, Santa Fe

The Santa Fe Opera archive volunteers, Bertram Heil, Roy Andrew Soskin

Staff of The Santa Fe Opera

INDEX

© 2006 The Santa Fe Opera
All rights reserved

**Library of Congress
Cataloging-in-Publication Data**

Huscher, Phillip.
The Santa Fe Opera:
　　an American pioneer /
　　by Phillip Huscher
p. cm.
Includes bibliographical
　　references and index.
ISBN-10: 0-86534-550-3
ISBN-13: 978-0-86534-550-8
　　(hardcover: alk. paper)
1. Santa Fe Opera. 2. Opera—
　　New Mexico—Santa Fe.
　　I. Title.

ML1711.8.S25H87 2006
792.509789'56–dc22
　　2006003108

Designed by
Jan Boleto

Technical design by
Michael Simpson

Color separations by
iocolor, Seattle

Produced by
Marquand Books, Inc.,
Seattle
www.marquand.com

Printed and bound by
CS Graphics Pte., Ltd.,
Singapore

Published by
The Santa Fe Opera
P. O. Box 2408
Santa Fe, NM 87504-2408
www.santafeopera.org

Distributed by
Sunstone Press, Santa Fe
www.sunstonepress.com